THE
PROPHECIES OF A
FATHER

To DR. Bentley
with deep
Appreciation for
your care over
my health.
HIE Eddie Turay.
June 2014,

THE PROPHECIES OF A FATHER

H.E. Ambassador Eddie M. Turay

authorHOUSE®

AuthorHouse™ UK Ltd.
1663 Liberty Drive
Bloomington, IN 47403 USA
www.authorhouse.co.uk
Phone: 0800.197.4150

Published by AuthorHouse   10/11/2013

ISBN: 978-1-4918-8081-4 (sc)
ISBN: 978-1-4918-8082-1 (e)

CONTENTS

I sincerely dedicate this book to the sweet memories of my benevolent parents. To my father, Paramount Chief Kande Turay, whose prophesies have come to pass! His prophesies made me who I am today. To my biological mother, Mrs Hawa Turay, and to my surrogate mother, Ya Warrah Kargbo, for her sincere motherly care and warmth. Her caring hands and compassion made me pull through after the untimely death of my biological mother. May their souls rest in perfect peace!

FOREWORD

This is the first autobiography written by a high commissioner serving Sierra Leone. It is very educative. It is written by someone who has seen and done it all, at the highest level of Sierra Leone's Judiciary Service, national politics, and diplomatic service. His Excellency Eddie Turay, currently the Sierra Leone High Commissioner to the Court of St James and nine other European countries, has successfully put together a brilliant piece that revolves around the prophecies of his father Paramount Chief (PC) Kande Turay of blessed memory.

By divine inspiration, the benevolent PC Kande saw in his son what it takes to dine and negotiate with royals, presidents, and prime ministers, at home and in faraway lands. These were the divine revelations, which compelled the writer to put his shoulder to the wheel and go for glory. And, to his delight, over the years these prophesies have come to pass. "These are amazing blessings!" the writer confirms and thanks the Creator of Heaven and Earth.

There is something unique about this book; the contents are very revealing and sincere. In addition to the revealing secrets of the author's traditional and parental background, he bravely states categorically that his late father was a non-believer.

For instance, in his day of eminence, Paramount Chief Kande Turay would place curses on those who stepped on his toes, and they suffered the ultimate penalties. The fact that the writer didn't shy away from what other writers might keep from their readers, is a manifestation of his forthrightness.

Not only that, the writer opens the readers' eyes to the colourful picture that surrounded the institution of Paramount Chieftaincy in those days. Sierra Leone has moved on since. We are talking about eighty years back in history. In those well-woven narratives, the writer creates and inspires a sense of difference between the cultural and traditional practices of that era and now.

He opens our eyes and minds further to another interesting character of his late father. He was an interesting paradox, which emphasises the critical twists in the narratives. Yes, Paramount Chief Kande Turay was a non-believer, and yet, he had admiration for all values that the Christian God and Western civilisation profess. Otherwise, why did he insist that his son, the writer, be educated in the Western way? Why did he allow him to attend Catholic mission schools? Why did he give the green light for his son's baptism in the Catholic faith? Why did he prevent the writer and his siblings from attending a Quranic institution?

Not once, not at any time, to the knowledge of the writer, did his benevolent dad decry the Whiteman as an enemy of the customs and traditions of his people and their ancestral spirits. Not once, to his knowledge, did his visionary dad decry the Whiteman and his civilisation for "putting a knife on the things, the values that held him and his subjects together" through Western education and Christianity.

In fact, his profound, love, respect, and admiration for its values have been made manifest in significant outcomes—the success stories and blessings of his son, HE Eddie Turay. Even in death, they have brought pride and happiness to PC Kande Turay and his late mothers.

The book throws significant light on the differences of Sierra Leone's political culture, under the single party political dispensation of President Siaka Stevens and the current system in this post-conflict era. The former was an era blighted by debilitating episodes, the writer reveals.

Typical of the former was his bitter experience with the political elites in Moyamba, where he worked as resident magistrate. Those were the dark ages of Sierra Leone's national politics, when the political crèmes called all the shots, sometimes at the expense of the civil liberties of senior civil servants holding different opinions.

Bravely, the author recalls with pride how he challenged the regime on that score. Amazingly, his bravery in defence of justice, democratic values, and human rights brought him to the attention of the president. It was amazing because it was typical of the president, then, to deal drastically with anyone (including the relatives of the president) identified by party loyalists as a disgruntled element or pragmatist, who failed to toe the party line.

Reflecting on the current government, the author paid tribute to the fruitful policies of President Ernest Bai Koroma, thereby cementing his loyalty to him. He acknowledges his generosity, care, and fortitude.

Pointing to a piece of crucial history in the political history of the New All People's Congress (APC), his party, the writer is thankful that he made the right decision and withdrew from the leadership race. He is thankful because at that crucial time, the party needed reconciliation, peace, and unity.

He has no regrets for withdrawing from that crucial APC leadership race for the 2007 polls in favour of the president. He regrets not, because it was revealed to him by an important man of God that Ernest Bai Koroma was the chosen leader of the party and would win the elections.

The Sierra Leone High Commission is arguably the most important of all our foreign missions. And the author enjoys his role there. He and his staff have contributed immensely to the invaluable task of uniting all Sierra Leoneans in this part of the diaspora. In like manner, he appreciates the contributions of his compatriots to national development at home.

This is an ideal text for educational institutions. Foreign and diplomatic service personnel and politicians at home and abroad will find this book not only useful but educative.

I have never read a book as frank as this one. I am very happy and proud to write the foreword, especially because this book was written by an important political figure, one of Sierra Leone's High Commissioners.

It is a good read!

Dr Michael N. Wundah
Senior Lecturer, Senior Examinations Expert
Lambeth Further Education College
London

ACKNOWLEDGEMENTS

Many people assisted with the writing of this book. Unfortunately, I can't afford to mention everybody by name, but I want to thank everyone for their contributions.

I want to sincerely thank His Excellency President Dr Ernest Bai Koroma for his support. I must admit that he contributed to the international aspects of the fulfilment of the prophecies of my late father by appointing me to serve as Sierra Leone's High Commissioner to the UK and eight other European countries. Members of our Great Party, the New All People Congress Party, deserve my special thanks.

Thanks to Dr Michael N Wundah, who proofread and edited the book and wrote the foreword. I want to acknowledge my secretary, Jeeva Ekanayake, for typing the manuscripts.

My family and loved ones deserve acknowledgements and thanks. Especially, I would like to acknowledge the collective contributions of my children as well as the encouragement of Daphine Iyamide Bajan Tejan-Sie.

I must confess that without them I couldn't have written this book. I would like my children to remember that this book tells their stories as well as mine, which I know they will be pleased to read.

Above all, I thank Almighty God for all He has done for me and my family. It was God who inspired and put me into remembrance to write comprehensively about all the events that have happened in my life, for the past sixty years. May the good Lord continue to guide and richly bless me, my entire family, and those who read this amazing book.

CHAPTER 1

REFLECTIONS

"Prophesies are divine, they come from above. They are communicated through divine inspirations. My case is a classic example. That my late father prophesied all that has come to past in my life, reminds me of an important salience. He was inspired by the Divine Master from above. It was that Master that put all the necessary jigsaws in place in order to make his prophecies come true."

The above quote reflects my father's perspective or version of the phrase prophecies. I often quote these words to people, including political and family gatherings. Amazingly, each time I say the above quotation to either people or myself, a certain peculiar feelings grip me and my thoughts go to my late father. The Great man was a genius as well as a visionary!

My father was a very powerful Paramount Chief. He ruled over many towns and villages which constituted his chieftain. My father was not a Ceremonial Ruler. He was crowned Paramount Chief by virtue of the customs and traditions of our chiefdom and clan. He reined for decades until he joined his ancestors on 23 October 1953.

There is one significant fact worth mentioning about my father. He was a traditional, natural ruler, which means that leadership runs through the veins of my late father's grandsires, their families, himself, and my own very veins and those of my siblings. I am not an expert in genetics, but it could be argued safely that the makeup of our genes undoubtedly accounts for leadership. I make this claim on the basis of my Christian background. As a Christian, I do recognise and hold dear to my heart that leadership, like authority, is divinely instituted.

My father was neither a soothsayer nor a phoney local magician. But, like all traditional rulers or Paramount Chiefs, especially during that era, my father owed his supernatural powers to the gods and ancestral spirits.[1] Therefore, he was obliged to rule and dispense his duties as directed by them. They were obligations my father couldn't ignore or defy. And this is why: they were obligations which constituted his natural and traditional rights. Being traditional and natural rulers distinguished them from ordinary mortals.

Yes, they were all-powerful, but Paramount Chiefs themselves owed their subjects certain obligations. It was part and parcel of Paramount Chiefs' traditional and customary rights and remits to mediate between the ancestral spirits, the gods of the land, and their subjects. They were obliged to protect and defend the realm and her people.[2]

Similarly, at all times and forevermore, the subjects owed Paramount Chiefs undivided and undisputed loyalty. They owed their lives and livelihood to their undisputed leaders, their Paramount Chiefs. Let us return to my father and his qualities, obligations, powers, and status.

I have to reiterate that his supernatural powers and relationship with the gods of the land and ancestral spirits made him unique. Through these powers as the interlocutor between the ancestral spirits, the gods, and his subjects, he interceded on their behalf for the former to fetch the land and its people rain, sun, and abundant fertility. It was his obligation to protect and defend his subjects and the land. Also, he was the Great Defender of the Faith of his people and the land.[3]

The customs and traditions which govern our clans and the institutions of Paramount Chieftaincy are stringent and straightforward. My father was the undisputed, celebrated mouthpiece of the gods and ancestral spirits. He was also the Chief Masquerade, in which capacity he participated in occultism, communicating with our ancestral spirits, demons, and mediums with various powers above and beyond the ordinary realm.[4]

Of course, those who are alien to our culture, traditions, and customs (I mean our ways of life and practices, generally speaking) may find this difficult to believe. Hence, I am very much aware of the fact that the phenomena I am talking about here are difficult to comprehend fully. Close to what makes sense of what I am trying to relay to you is the concept of metaphysics.[5]

Even at that, I do know one thing. Mainstream religions and their believers would doubt the credibility of our ways and practices at that time, let alone comprehend fully and believe and practice them. But the fact of the matter is that every nation has her system, culture, and practices. Every nation and race has their faith which defines their national character.

Put simply, for the non-initiate or novitiates of our customs, traditions, culture, and beliefs, this may sound strange. It is cumbersome to make sense of the logic and inherent powers, traditions, and customary roles of typical rulers in the period under discussion. Hence, my father's extraordinary powers would confuse you, but being one of his 120 children, brought into this world by one of his 60 wives, I speak within the range of neither exaggeration, nor spin, but the absolute truth.

Again, you may bemused and baffled by the numbers of wives and children my dad had. His wives were neither harems nor concubines. In fact, as a matter of our traditions and customs, some of his wives, my mothers, were betrothed unto him. The others, including my mother, he wooed, or according to the profound cliché, he chose them as his wives. My late mother fell in the second category, a category of royal with the mark, blessings of romantic manifestations and grace.

3

It is educative to note that this cultural practice varies. Things were different in other clans, according to their customs, traditions, and cultural practices, especially in those days prior to the colonial era. Wives were won on battlefields. They constituted booty, the spoils of warfare for the victorious camp.

In those days, traditional rulers wielded enormous powers over their subjects. That doesn't mean that they were all autocrats and dictators. They governed peacefully according to the norms and values handed down to them by the gods and ancestral spirits.

Some Paramount Chiefs, including my father, were also extremely rich, because their sources of wealth were in abundance and could be readily cultivated. But the volume of wealth was dependent on the resources at the PC's disposal. Some wealth, hegemony, were achieved through conquest.[6]

Wealth and its sources were absolutely clean; warfare and conflict over terrain were legitimate endeavours. The vices of greed and avarice, selfishness and self-centredness were condemned as anathemas. The PCs were expected to share the proceeds of their wealth with their subjects and, above all, the gods and ancestral spirits.

Hence, it was the case that wealth, whether small or massive, wasn't begotten through dubious practices or means. The vices of bribery and corruption, as we know them today, were deemed taboos; they were anathemas and therefore against the laws of the land.[7]

My father was a very fortunate ruler. As they say in the popular, traditional cliché, the Great One was indeed blessed by the gods and his ancestral spirits. He ruled over a vast dynasty, a dynasty he and his subjects fought for and won through conquest. That made him one of the wealthiest and most powerful rulers in the region during the period under discussion.

The institutions of Paramount Chiefs and the laws and powers which govern them were deemed sacred. The institutions were well structured and ordered according to the customs and traditions of the land. The compositions of modern Paramount Chieftaincy institutions differ from the pre-colonial and colonial eras. In modern times, depending on region, chieftaincy is hereditary.

The institution of Paramount Chieftaincy could also be patriarchal or matriarchal, depending on the chieftain variation. The leadership or administrative structure could equally be similar to that of a pyramid, at the top or apex of which is the Paramount Chief, flanked by his deputy, speaker, senior chiefs, assistant chiefs and their deputies, section chiefs, town chiefs, village chiefs, and their local councillors.[8]

That I am very much conscious and glued to the status and history of my clan and region of origin makes me not less an internationalist, nor does it deem me the typical non-receptive nationalist or an ultranationalist.

I am a bona fide, patriotic Sierra Leonean and a proud ethnic Temne. History has it that Temnes were traditionally organised into about fifty chiefdoms, each led by a chief, called *Bai* in the Temne language. The British later called this leader the **Bai,** Paramount Chief. With the passage of time, some of the larger chiefdoms were constituted into sections. Each large village or group of smaller villages had its own untitled sub-chief.

Each village also had an elected headman. In the chief's villages, there usually resided four to six titled chiefs. These titled chiefs served their chief as advisors and facilitators. One of them was very important; usually called *"Kapri me ʃe m,"* he served as the interim ruler in a likely caretaker government role after the demise of the chief.

So that raises the question: Who determined the members of the institution's pyramid-like organisation? To reiterate, saying that the institution of Paramount Chieftaincy was well-organised is an understatement. Every chief was entitled by customs and traditions (and the powers vested in him by the gods) to choose his own sub-chiefs. At his coronation (or installation), they are installed with him. And this part of our customs and traditions are different from other ethnic groups, regions, and clans in Sierra Leone. We may be of

5

the same nationality, but there are distinct traditional, customary, and cultural practices which differentiate us.

In Temne land, in those days, each sub-chief, titled or not, selected a sister's daughter as his helper. In Temne language, the selected daughter is known as the *"mankapr."* Also, each of the chiefs selected one or more sister's daughters to help him. These female sub-chiefs only had "ritual" not "administrative" duties of this all-powerful institution.

With the proclamation of the Protectorate by the British in 1896, the chiefdoms became units of local government. The chiefs were placed on stipends and became low-level administrative bureaucrats. Smaller chiefdoms were amalgamated into single units or fewer, economically viable and manageable entities. They were answerable to the colonial district commissioners (DCs).

History has it that my clan is rooted in Sanda in the Bombali District, Northern Region of Sierra Leone. My father often reminded me about my roots during his quiet moments outside the glare of other people's eyes and ears. I must warn that they had no xenophobic connotations. To which end, I must emphasise that I have strong leanings and ties with my compatriots from other districts, regions, and ethnicities, and of different political persuasions and beliefs.

My homeland, the place I truly call home, is Sierra Leone. It comprises villages, towns, chiefdoms, districts, and regions. I talk of districts and regions here because Sierra Leone was configured along such lines after it was subjugated to colonialism.[9]

My homeland is a former British colony with a rich history. The Portuguese had set foot here, but it was only by way of naming the country, and their stay was brief. The shoreline looked like the shape of a lion to the Portuguese explorer, Pedro Da Cintra, and in 1462, he named the land "Sierra Lyoa" ("Lion Mountains" in Portuguese). Sixteenth-century English sailors called it "Sierra Leoa"; by the seventeenth century, it was "Sierra Leona"; and in 1787, under British rule, it became Sierra Leone.[10]

What is the genesis of the history of this historic place, my illustrious homeland, called Sierra Leone, the Province of Freedom? In the 1780s, the number of freed slaves in London grew, as a result of actions such as Sharp's in the 1772 case of James Somerset. The question was where they should best live and be employed. Sharp's answer was that they should settle in the continent from which they (or their ancestors) came.[11]

By agreement with a local chief of the Temne tribe, known to the British as King Tom, twenty miles of hilly coast were secured for the purpose (they are situated between the mouths of two notorious slaving rivers, the Sierra Leone and the Sherbro). Here there arrived from London, in 1787, a naval vessel carrying 331 freed slaves, 41 of them women, and somewhat confusing the issue in philanthropic terms, 60 white London prostitutes.[12]

The settlement got up to a disastrous start. Half the settlers died in the first year. Several of the freed slaves opted for a prosperous new life working for local slave traders. And King Tom's successor, King Jimmy, attacked and burnt the settlement in 1789. But it was rebuilt on a new site and given the name Freetown.[13]

This new settlement was dubbed the Province of Freedom. It was a little known peninsula then that only covered an area known as Freetown. It means that the geographical size of Sierra Leone was only limited to Freetown. During that time, a British trading company administered the territory.

After years of disagreement, the ownership and administration of the territory was handed over to a British colonial administration. They stepped in and ruled the country for four hundred years. Throughout the four hundred years of British colonialism, the suzerainty set out to configure a colonial administrative system suited to the rationale of the colonial project: divide and rule and gain economic advantage.[14]

The little known peninsula, Freetown, was declared a Crown Colony in 1808. And in 1896, the hinterland was also declared a British protectorate for economic reasons.

It is in the belly of this hinterland that the secret of the story of my entire generation lies. I will skip it for now and come back to it later.

The two separate entities, colony and protectorate, were reconfigured into one state and later granted independence on 27 April 1961. The protectorate was organised into administrative chiefdoms, administered by British district commissioners. These chiefdoms and their districts are inhabited by ethnic groups. There are thirteen ethnic groups in Sierra Leone. Sanda, the chiefdom of my birth, is one of the chiefdoms.[15]

British colonialism brought Westernisation to my home country, Sierra Leone: education, culture, and Christianity, and even acquired affluence. But what it didn't bring was the abundant gifts Mother Nature gave freely to this land.

In 2011, the former British prime minister, Rt. Honourable Tony Blair, spoke about Sierra Leone. Blair is a true friend and promoter of Sierra Leone on the international stage. As patron of the Africa Governance Initiative (AGI), he and his partners have sustained and consolidated the peace, which he helped to broker.

Blair said, "Sierra Leone also has incredible natural resources: an abundance of minerals, beautiful beaches, rich arable land, fisheries, the third largest natural harbour in the world, and above all, a real entrepreneurial mind-set."[16]

My father was not only a gifted person who could accurately prophesy the future, he was also a solid storyteller. His storylines were rooted in fables; they always kept me awake. I loved listening to him and his stories, for they taught me to be wise at an early age. One evening in his throne room, he sat me down and narrated the history of my Sanda, our Sanda.

According to my father, in the early part of my ancestral history, Sanda was predominantly inhabited by ethnic groups known as the Lokos and Limbas. Unlike the areas often exploited for political gains, this area was not part of the Temne habitats. The Temnes were found in the areas covering Tinkolili District, notably in the Taneh area.

The area inhabited by the Lokos and Limbas was vast. It stretched from Pamlap, near Makeni, hovering across vast lands, from Foru Loko area, to Kamaranka, down to Kamalo and Kamakwie, to Sella, close to the Guinea border. Vast landownership had its inherent benefits and wider ramifications. Landownership on a large scale meant wielding real political power among the various clans and even beyond, covering the other regions.[17]

Also, it meant wielding economic power and commanding huge households who would work on the lands and tend their cattle. These two groups created the Limba and Loko dynasties. They had rights to their separate chieftains with their necessary traditional and customary rights to accession and succession. There were defined rights over landownership, subsistence farming, and cattle grazing rights, which often created flashpoints, tensions between the two ethnic groups.

There was a semblance of an amicable co-existence between the Lokos and Limbas. However, beneath the surface of this so-called amicable relationship, there were fundamental tensions ignited by landownership and cattle grazing. I must emphasise that these were not mere conflicts which could have been settled in courts or by the elders. Now and again, they would lead to real ethnic feuds and wars, resulting in massive damage to property and loss of lives.[18]

It came to a time when the conflict between the Lokos and Limbas was persistent, and it led to an all-out war between the two groups. There were many such wars, and some were fought fiercely, creating deep-seated enmity among the warring protagonists, the warlords, and the ruling clans. For instance, one such brutal war occurred prior to the declaration of the British protectorate over the hinterland.

As the war raged on, it became apparent that the Lokos were losing the battle to the Limbas. The realisation dawned on them that it would spell out tragedy if they became too complacent over their predicament, so they had no choice but to seek external help and forge an alliance, or else they would be forced to surrender to the Limbas. They considered any form of surrender to the Limbas as an anathema, a taboo. They couldn't imagine becoming prisoners of war as substitute for war indemnities.

It is instructive to reiterate that the Limba and the Loko dynasties and the lands over which they exercised authority were vast. The advantages which emanated from owning vast lands were huge. They entailed economic benefits in addition to the power and authority the chiefs wielded. No doubt, some chiefs were eager to wage war against their neighbours, especially the ones considered weak or feeble, so as to accumulate more lands. Also, the defeated on the battlefield were forced to pay tributes to their victor's suzerainty and part and parcel of war indemnities.

At the time of the Loko-Limba war, the Lokos occupied areas spanning from Makeni, Pamlap, Foru Loko, to Batkanu. The Limba dynasty covered areas from Safroko, Briwa, and right down to areas in Kamalo to Kamakwie and Sella. The areas that Limbas inhabited are known today as Briwa-Limba Brima-Sanda in the Port Loko District, constituting the whole of Matherkerma. These are the amalgamated chiefdoms of Gbanti-Kamaranka.[19]

When the war reached fever pitch, the Lokos found a new ally in the Taneh region in Tonkolili District. That ally was Pa Ker-Wokle, the famous, fearsome, fearless, and powerful Temne war lord. The purpose of the alliance was obvious: to assist the Lokos in pushing the Limbas out of the territories they had seized during the conflict. At that time, the Limbas had already taken areas in Fouray-Loko, Mateboi, right down to Rokulan-Kamaranka (now Gbanti Kamaranka Chiefdom) to Kamalo, joining through Sella Limba.

Warlords have special meanings in African traditions and customs. To assume the title of a warlord during the time under discussion was not for novice. Like traditional leadership, in those days when Africa was a virgin land, some people had the status of warlord bestowed on them, and others earned it through inheritance; ancestors often hand over all that it takes to be a powerful warlord in a mysterious dream.[20]

Either way, a warlord must prove his capability, prowess, at the crucible, that is, on the battlefield. Warlords were not only very important, they were perceived as having extraordinary powers. Traditional African religion upholds that like traditional rulers or natural rulers, the warlords, chief priests, chief hunters, masquerades, heads, and facilitators of secret societies such as the Bundoo, Poro, Gbaganni, Korfo, Wayde, or Waydei were the mouthpieces of the gods and the ancestral spirits.

Warlords were treated with such awe that they occupied a special place in African traditions, customs, and spirituality. Whatever they suggested to the chiefs was taken seriously. Call it one of those infinite fables, but some of the warlords who later went on to become renowned chiefs were said to have supernatural powers. They could disguise themselves—turn into predatory animals or disappear in the face of fierce enemy attacks—and of course, they had bulletproof vests made of powerful charms.[21]

Pa Ker-Wokle[22] was a special warlord with extraordinary supernatural powers and valour in our chiefdoms. His track record on the battlefield was awesome; he fought on behalf of his people in so many successful battles. They were not only won, they surpassed all the other wars won by his contemporaries in the region. He was renowned for having extra powers which made him invincible in battle. Also, he was wealthy and had harems of wives offered to him as bride prizes, according to customs and traditions.

He agreed to fight on behalf of the Lokos, and his Temne warriors pushed the Limbas from Fouray-Loko right down to the perimeter of Kamakwie, where they are settled to this day. The areas the Limbas occupied before the push covered Sanda Tenraren, Sanda Tegbonko, Sanda Loko, and Mathen Kerma. After the integration of these areas, they were known as Kareneh District, with headquarters at Batkanu, in the Gbendu Gowahum Chiefdom. They were amalgamated and became the present day Bombali District, with headquarters in Makeni.[23]

The battle was fought fiercely and won on behalf of the Lokos. When the dusts of war settled, the great warrior Pa Ker-Wokle and his footmen and soldiers were entreated to stay in the liberated areas to a place called, in the local Temne dialect, *"Ro-gbaneh"* (a meeting place or place where people gather).

Pa Ker-Wokle had many affable qualities in addition to his valour, and his troops were disciplined. They were not the typical mercenaries or retainers who would trade their services through their military might and weight behind a hirer, largely because of financial gains. This great warrior had principles, and so there was finesse and professionalism in the way he operated.

Due to these qualities, he and his troops were highly regarded; they were invited to settle for good in Ro-gbaneh Township. He was offered a wife in appreciation of his military service to the Loko Dynasty, meaning that he was no longer a stranger or mercenary. He became part and parcel of the Lokos and their dynasty. The fierce warrior and his entire clan moved from Taneh to Sanda Tegbonkoh (now Gbanti Kamaranka Chiefdom after the amalgamation).[24]

The story of Pa Ker-Wokle, the brave warrior, is significant in the context of my story for two reasons. His descendants included Pa Gbominoh, Pa Fishar, and my father, Pa Lacomm, who later became a Paramount Chief. This means that I hailed from a strong line of warrior chiefs.[25]

That my father later became Paramount Chief of Sanda was due to the valour of Pa Ker-Wokle. During my father's reign, Sierra Leone was still under British imperial rule. My father inherited his tenacity, valour, fearlessness, and strong leadership qualities from Pa Ker-Wokle.

As stated inter alia, in addition to their spiritual, traditional roles, Paramount Chiefs played dual roles. On one hand, they represented the voice of their subjects. On the other, they mediated between their subjects and the British Crown's representatives, the district commissioners. There was mutual respect between the two partners,

PCs and DCs. Hence they officially addressed each other in their official communications, including memos, as "My good friend."[26]

I would implore the reader not to read too much into this so-called "mutual trust" and "respect" between Her Majesty's Colonial District Commissioners and their so-called "good friends," the PCs. It was superficial, ceremonial, just in name. Look at it this way: most PCs were illiterate; secondly, they were subjects of Her Majesty and the very DCs. There was nothing like parity in terms of power and authority.

Hence, the phrase "My good friend" was a mere front, a diplomatic cliché. It was beautifully shrouded in a cheap diplomatic language in order to disguise the inherent disparities which characterised the relationship. The essence was to create an amicable atmosphere to enable the colonial power to create and govern a relationship that was predicated on gross inequality in the real sense of the word.

The administration of Her Majesty's protectorate territories and colonies was well organised. There were regular meetings between PCs and their district commissioners. The former chaired the meetings. For example, my father and all the Paramount Chiefs in the district used to attend meetings presided over by the district commissioner.

District commissioners were treated like demigods, and indeed that was what they exactly were. All their official meetings with their PCs were accompanied by pomp and pageantry. Paramount Chiefs were accompanied to these meetings by traditional dancers and musicians.

My father was not prone to unnecessary distractions. He possessed an acute business-like mind. That was not all; my father may not have been an educated person, but he had special listening and critical thinking skills. He was always very attentive at their regular meetings with the district commissioner.

And I must say that looking back on those days, and the stories he told me, I want to believe that my father admired education and the educated. I hold this view because most of the DCs assigned to the colonies in those days were very young, and yet they were given such huge responsibility and accorded unique accolades.

My father was a visionary. He must have marvelled at the reasons behind that, and in his quiet moments, he must have realised that those young men were assigned to such important posts because they were educated. The level of education not really important, but since they were DCs, they were perceived as highly educated officials of the Crown.

At one of their usual official meetings with the DC, my father went with his dancers and musicians as part of his huge entourage. Little did he know that at that particular meeting, he would come in contact with the woman who was destined to be his future wife, and my mother. On the very day he arrived, he met one sergeant major.

Sergeant Major Bengi was from Gbendembu Gowahun Chiefdom. He was the senior court messenger in the district office. Both men became good friends, and to further cement this friendship, Sergeant Major Bengi ordered food to be prepared and asked one of his daughters to take it to Paramount Chief Kande Turay (my father). The young lady sent on that special errand was Hawa, my mother-to-be.

My mother's beauty dazzled my father and knocked him off his feet. It was the typical love at first sight; my father sought her hand in marriage immediately. He paid a token as the bride price, just for formality sake. As PC, customs demanded that his wishes wouldn't be denied him. Readily, Sergeant Major Bengi accepted my dad's proposal, and he and my mother became husband and wife. Thus, I am made up of the knack, tenacity, valour, and bravery of my father and his ancestors, and the meek, angelic, and compassionate heart of my late mother.[27]

My father revealed to me one day that that particular meeting was one of the finest and historic moments in his life as Paramount Chief. He confessed to me in these words: "I went to attend a conference with the DC and I ended up with a wife. I shall never forget that day. I felt fulfilled because I felt an urgent love, passion for your mother the moment she handed the food to me."[28]

Consumed by love and romantic passion, my father was desperate. He did not waste any further time, because he was eager to have my mum by his side as his new bride. Thus, at the end of the conference, he took his new bride, my mother, home with him to our village of Rogbanti. From that moment, my mum assumed the status of one of my father's sixty wives.

Polygamy is an age-old custom in Africa. Some argue that it has endured to this day due to necessity. Since the African male has to rely on subsistence farming for his livelihood, he needs to increase the labour force. As many wives as possible are required in any man's household in order to increase the yields of his farm: rice and coffee, cocoa, piassava, ginger, pepper, cassava plantations. Others argue that polygamy persists in Africa due to the African male's predatory sexual instincts.

Population analysts and some sociologists have different lines of arguments on this matter. Some argue that polygamy is borne out of the fact that there are more women in the population than men. And hence, in order to avoid promiscuity, the one man-one wife philosophy would be unhelpful, as young women who lack suitors and husbands in their lives would resort to promiscuity or prostitution.

Others argue that polygamy, especially among natural rulers, and generally among African men, is considered one of their countless God-given rights. Thus, they have the right to exercise it freely, without fear or favour. And amazingly, it is accepted by some women as the norm.

Like my dad said, I was born with something special about me. Most profound is the indisputable fact that I was born with the precision and discipline of my father. I was born in his true likeness and image, which I am very proud of and grateful for. My father remains as I saw him. He still remains a towering, dignified, graceful figure. He always walked with his shoulders and head gallantly above everyone.

Yes, he joined his forefather decades ago, but I avowedly say, from the depths of my thoughts, that nothing, absolutely nothing has changed my perceptions about him. And, by the Grace of God, the Maker of Heaven and Earth, so shall it be, so shall he remain forever and evermore, deep in the infinite stretch of my thoughts and memory!

Sometime when I reflect on the life and character of my late father, I still visualise him, the way he used to speak, give commands to his subjects, his wives, and us, his beloved 120 children. I still visualise the manner in which he used to admonish and adjudicate fairly and justly in his majestic, chiefly chambers.

Most important of all, the Great Man forged a great bond between himself and his subjects. There was warmth and goodwill between him and everyone, rich or poor. I am proud to state that I have inherited these values and vow to guide and defend my people at all times.

My father was right that I am a special child. Indeed I am a special child! And this is why. Just few months after my mother married my dad, she was pregnant with her first and only child. I am that child. My father named me *"Pioor"* or *"Popiyoh,"* meaning "the Bright One" or "the Brilliant One."

There is more to my name. It represents the name of a powerful "demon." I was later made to understand from one of my stepmothers that my father chose this particular name for me because he believed that I was going to grow into someone special.[29]

That stepmother gave me hope and a new lease on life. Her name was Ya Warrah Kargbo; later, she became my surrogate mother. She assumed this role after the premature death of my biological mother, seven days after I was born. Ya Warrah Kargbo represented nothing other than a very caring, generous, and warm personality.

In retrospect, I must confess that Ya Warrah Kargbo was unlike my other stepmothers. She treated me like her own biological son, especially since I was not old enough to know, let alone remember, my real mother. Unfortunately, Ya Warrah Kargbo was barren, meaning she wasn't blessed with the fruits of the womb. And this secret was revealed to me when I became of age, for, as I said inter alia, I was only seven days old when my biological mother met her tragic death.

Ya Warrah Kargbo shared with me the secret connotation of my name when I was about ten; I could hear the other stepmothers who were close to me whisper to each other, "He is the Bright One, the Brilliant One, the Blue Eye, our husband." I didn't understand what they said and the real meaning of the special name our father chose for me.

But with the passage of time, I matured, entered secondary school, and sat to my Ordinary Levels examinations, and then I gained the realisation. First, I easily attracted authority and could easily gain favours from other people. It often happened naturally, smoothly, to the extent that I myself was sometimes baffled by some of the favours I enjoyed with ease.

It is not any fault of mine that I can't remember one-third of my stepmothers by name, let alone say the names of all sixty of them. Amazingly, even they themselves (stepmothers) didn't know each other by name. Having said that, I still remember the names of some of my stepmothers, especially those who took good care of me on the orders of my surrogate mother and father. I

If there is anything I should remember forever, including the names of people who were prominent in my formative years, they are my magnanimous stepmothers. Yes, there were sixty of them in number, but the prominent names I still remember are Ya Boinki, Ya Bumposeh, Ya Ruggie, and Ya Gbaysay. To reiterate, I still remember because they played pivotal roles in my formative years, for which I shall ever be grateful.

I am a *"Destiny Child,"* a typical survivor. I say so because at the premature death of my biological mother, seven days after my birth, I was left to survive at the expense and generosity of the breast milk of my stepmothers. My father chose Ya Warrah Kargbo; I was put in her care, and he instructed her to take good care of me. My father ingeniously chose her and gave her this massive and important task. I think my dad made this significant choice because Ya Warrah Kargbo was my mother's most trusted mate and best friend.

Although there is hardly any love lost between mates, and they are usually bitter rivals and always locked horns over their husband, Ya Warrah Kargbo was a special case. She was different; she virtually begged and pleaded with my other stepmothers, her fellow mates, to breastfeed me in turns. In this regard, she told me one day, "I used to take you from one stepmother to the other when you were seven days old in order to breastfeed you in turns."[30]

You would agree with me that it was a peculiar situation, and once in a while conflict would arise. No matter how generous my stepmothers would have liked to be, human nature being what it is, sometimes fluid, my personal circumstance was often marred by disagreements among my stepmothers.

I must confess that inasmuch as I owe a lot to all of my stepmothers, I owe more gratitude to my surrogate mother. She was everything to me: my counsel, my best friend. She was the only personality of all my stepmothers I confided in.

Regarding the significance and peculiarity of my name, my surrogate mother revealed a secret to me which I ponder over to this day. I ponder over the revelation, considering the fact that my father gave me the opportunity that exposed me to the other side: faith in God through Christianity ever since I went to school.

My surrogate mother whispered that I was named after a kind of deity, one of my father's demons or mediums. Pondering over the rationale behind naming me after a demon, I wondered why my dad sent me to school, where I was taught a religion contrary to the very demon after which he named me.

Amazingly, I was not the only child that our father named after those demons or mediums. Each of my siblings was named after a specific demon or medium. My siblings' names, including Sonthi, Kulokoh,

Ballaeh, and Gbominoh, derived from demonic names in the spirit world.

African polygamous homes are not uniform; they differ in so many ways. There is a link between polygamy and social status. For instance, women in polygamous homes of Paramount Chiefs and the homes of financially well-off men suffer less in terms of the fulfilment of their needs.

In poorer homes, for instance, households manned by poor subsistence farmers or men in low-paid manual jobs, polygamy hits their women very hard. Because my father was a PC, his wives, my stepmothers, lived happily and didn't bother about their livelihoods. They were well cared for, and like their husband, they occupied a special position in society.

Atheism is not peculiar to a particular culture or nation. As I grew older, I learnt that my father was an atheist. He never prayed in a mosque or church. He was an atheist, but with a difference.

Having said that, it doesn't mean that my father had no faith; maybe he was constrained by the traditional status he occupied in society. Thus, he might be at ease with polytheism, communicating and being at ease with demons, devil, spirits, and mediums. But he didn't look less on the strength of other faiths. He neither despised nor banished Christians out of his chiefdom because of their faith. He encouraged his subjects to live side-by-side with people of all faiths and beliefs.

It is fair to argue that situational ethics might have had a grip on my father. He had extraordinary powers and could invoke evil spirits and demons to cast woes and calamities on his enemies. He could cast evil spells and put a curse on those who stepped on his toes. And the curses he placed on people always had devastating effects, so he was respected and feared by his fellow chiefs as well as his subjects.

My siblings and I opened our eyes to the rich culture of our clan. The one I enjoyed most was the communal eating. In a big bowl of calabash, we were assembled to eat the family meals as united princes of Paramount Chief Kande Turay, our darling father.

The assembly eating point (or what might be called a dining room) was in my father's Court Barrie. In the history of African customs and tradition, it is the meeting point or arena preserved for men. My sisters and stepmothers only entered my dad's Court Barrie and its inner chambers if there was a pressing need. It was profane for females to sit there and chat with the men.

In my father's Court Barrie (what is known in modern times as a courtroom), all manner of disputes, ranging from petty thieving to serious criminal cases, were judged. They were decided by my father and his senior chiefs and courtiers. As one of his sons, and the chosen one at that, it was my right to sit in my father's Court Barrie in judgment. In my dad's Court Barrie, I opened my eyes to what you may call grandiose power politics. It was controlled by potent authority. It was controlled and managed by my father, the Paramount Chief, and his sub-chiefs and courtiers.

It was in that same Court Barrie that I first felt the power and authority of politics. Power, I was taught in the arena of my father's Court Barrie, is authority, it is wealth, and it is powerful. But I was taught something important in that arena. I was taught to believe faithfully that political power is transient. Hence, when it is time for power to go to the next person, to change hands, don't pose unnecessary hurdles or obstacles on the way.

My father told me, "Since you receive it gracefully, learn to bow out as gracefully as you received it."

I asked, "What if you received it on the battlefield?"

He smiled and replied, "Of course, you still do. Remember, power and authority is still liquid. It is as solid as a rock."

I was curious and asked, "You speak in riddles, parables. What do you mean, Daddy?"

He laughed and then explained further, "What I mean to say is simple. Whether power is won on the battlefield, or given to you in a dream or on a silver plate, it is laden with the flames of fire."

It was in my dad's Court Barrier that I was inspired to read and practice law and aspire for politics. It was in that arena that I realised that laws and politics are correlated. I also discovered that the laws of the land are there to defend and protect politics, only when politics carries the weight of grace.

Jeremy Paxman, in his text *The Political Mal*, commented, "Living in a political household where politics is the daily diet introduces the child to the excitement of political life early on."

But there was a difference. In my father's household and courtroom, I was made to believe at an early age that violence, intimidation, lies, intrigue, cheating, and betrayal have no place in politics that is blessed with grace.

I was made to understand, by virtue of all that transpired in that small but mighty in valour arena, that power is divinely instituted. I learned in that arena that power and authority are built on the pillars of the truth, fairness, justice, and faith.

Above all, I learned scores of lessons in my father's court chambers. In those chambers of political power, I was inspired to reckon that power and politics favours listening ears and undivided, attentive skills. I realised that power and authority without grace is empty and fruitless; it is cursed. Truly, I learned that power without grace is doomed.

There is no society in which there isn't a class system, rigid, flexible, or mild. Of course, elitism and class systems prevailed during the reign of my father, and it does exist to this day, but it wasn't as tense, rigid, cruel, divisive, and destructive to the extent that it created the atmosphere for an apartheid system and culture. And to this day, there is no apartheid or xenophobic culture in Sierra Leone. Intermarriage was encouraged among the elite members of the ruling houses or clans and the working class. Thankfully, as I write this book, the culture of inclusiveness, though sometimes manipulated by greedy politics, exists throughout the length and breadth of Sierra Leone.

Paramount Chiefs consolidated their status and their grip on power by creating alliances. Some of the alliances were forged through intermarriages between dynastic members. There were other norms and values, customary and traditional, which held our clan together. They included male and female circumcision rites. But above these rituals, there was the higher level referred to as the "Male Poro Society," symbolised by their various masks and masquerades. *"Kpagbani,"* one of the awesome masquerades, has a lot to do with the spirit world.[31]

The society and culture that my father was made Paramount Chief over knew justice and fairness as the pillars of unity. It knew that the law of the land needed support to function fairly and justly. In fact, it wasn't only in our area, but the whole of Temne land adhered to these virtuous values. Temne clans do reckon that these sacred values are the very cradle of our civilisation and culture.

Kenneth Wylie, among others, paints graphic portraits of what he called the social control of the Temne:

"Among nineteenth-century Temne, the law did not have the preeminent place in the resolution of disagreements and conflicts in the way court systems do in twentieth-century democracies. There was no separate, largely independent judiciary; socio-political leaders tried certain cases as a prerogative of their position. Rather than applying abstract ideals of justice, equity, and good conscience, these leaders made decisions in light of the particular political and social settings in each separate instance. Disagreements and conflicts between individuals and groups were adjudicated at, first, the kin-group and residence-group level, second, at the association level (especially the Poro and Boodo societies), and third, at the chiefdom and sub-chiefdom level (in a chief's court). The first level used primarily moot proceedings, the second usually inquisitor techniques, and at the third level, a kind of adversarial contest. In the colonial court system only courts of those chiefs recognised as Paramount Chiefs served as local courts. A modified system of this model continues to this day" (Wylie, 1977).

The beauty about this carefully designed system of justice is that it was meticulous. Justice and fairness were virtues, which were not thwarted by the chiefs. In all this, they did consult their ancestral spirits and the gods when deemed necessary. Again, these practices varied from ethnic group to ethnic group and from region to region in Temne land.

There is so much talk of jurisprudence as obtained in modernity, but the system described above had clear elements of it. By and large, it depended on the custodian of justice — the chiefs. The manner in which they adjudicated the laws for their subjects went a long way to show who they were and how they perceived justice and fairness naturally. So the individual differences of chiefs was the key factor.

These rituals described by Wylie are not as popular as they used to be, sixty years ago, when my siblings and I were teenagers, and during the period my father was on the throne. As time went on, they were submerged and wiped out by Christian and Islamic beliefs. Like in other regions of Sierra Leone, the two mainstream religions have won a lot of converts. They have done so successfully through concrete and influential mediums.

By the beginning of the mid-fifties (and some records would say even prior to that), the Wesleyan Methodist and Catholic missions had meandered their way into the traditional hubs of society in Temne land. They won converts covering every village, town, chiefdom, and district in the province of Temne land.

They did so through their educational institutions. Other means or instruments of conversion were the needed social services, including public and community health services. In particular, Islam cut down drastically on the hitherto influences of polytheism, animism, atheism, and paganism. Quranic schools, madrasas, and mosques have impacted people and their lives in our region as well as elsewhere in Sierra Leone.

To this day, some of those who are faithful to this system of belief, either because they were born in it or because they were converted to it, look back on the decline in the power and influence of their deities and rituals with dismay. They decried the sea change that set to dislodge the traditional and spiritual beliefs of their forefathers and their ancestral spirits. To some it is profane, an anathema, a taboo, an abomination. To those converts who are at ease with their newfound religion and beliefs, it is time to fall in love with the Age of Enlightenment and postmodernism.

The manner in which the traditional diehards condemned the sea change when they looked back on those days is similar in many ways to the prolific writer, Nobel Laureate Chinua Achebe, of blessed memory. In his popular piece *Things Fall Apart*, he wrote, "The white man is very clever. He came quietly and peacefully with his religion. He has put a knife on the things that held us together. Our clan can longer act as one, and things are falling apart."[32]

I am not in any way attempting to discredit the position of the late Chinua Achebe. After all, he was one of the finest minds, with such a huge literary capacity in Africa, if not in the entire world. But one can counter this view. And as for me, I seriously believe that Christianity is one of the serenest gifts of the Age of Enlightenment.

And in view of her critical comments on the manner in which the world views and the Age of Enlightenment are connoted and perceived, Susan Neiman stated, "The disenchantment of the world is one thing, the demystification of human nature quite another. The more your own secrets are uncovered, the more you may feel that there's no self left at all" (Neiman, 2009, 120-138).

Mine is a salient argument and not a criticism of Achebe, as stated inter alia. My position: If we weigh and contrast the opinions of his people in the context of their cultures, traditions, practices, rituals (polytheism, couched in deities, et al.), and the new and fresh lights which were brought in the wake of the Age of Enlightenment, I would stick with the latter. This is one of the core reasons why I am a Christian and believer. To me, Christianity and its credos signify one of the redemptive projects of the Age of Enlightenment.

CHAPTER 2

EARLY EDUCATION IN GBANTI VILLAGE

———◦———

"To acknowledge the value of education, it is worth
trying illiteracy for a second. The reality is that with
education, there is always a second chance. Education
has the capacity to conquer ignorance, hunger, and
disease. There is always the possibility to be on top of
the world."

The Chronicles of a Roman Elite

Illiteracy emerges as part and parcel of people's lives in many ways.
For some, it is not by choice. Circumstances beyond their control
relegate them to the dark world of illiteracy. For this group of victims,
if I may call them so, illiteracy is imposed on them. It could also be
argued that others are made illiterate by choice. They may have had
the opportunity to gain education and improve their lot, but had
misused the chance and opportunity. The cultures and perceptions of
certain milieus also bring illiteracy to bear on people.

Regarding the reason behind my father's illiteracy, there is hardly any
explanation as to why he was illiterate. All I can say with certainty is
that although he occupied one of the most powerful positions in the

history of our local and tradition politics, he could neither read nor write. He was, however, very intelligent and an acute visionary.

In retrospect, you could argue that my father was an illiterate, but he didn't go to illiteracy, nor did it come to him by choice. Undoubtedly, this genius of a traditional ruler knew the value of education. The education that we are talking about was perceived by many of his kind as the Whiteman's education, couched in the image and values of the Whiteman and his white world.

With confidence, I speak on this very important matter of socialisation for my late father. Certainly, he didn't perceive education as exclusively the cultural values and knowledge bases of the Whiteman. He was not rebellious against education because it is the critical mass and science of the Whiteman.

Here is my concrete justification to support this premise. If he didn't know the value of education, he wouldn't have refused to send me to the Quranic school in order to learn the Quran. Thankfully, through divine inspiration, the Great Man chose to send me and my siblings to the Whiteman's school in order to acquire a Western education.

Sierra Leone's national history will tell you that my father was not the only Paramount Chief who was illiterate. In those days—between the 1930s and the 1950s—most of the Paramount Chiefs in Sierra Leone, as well as in other parts of Africa, were illiterate. There were only a handful of educated Paramount Chiefs.

I must point out that illiteracy among traditional rulers or Paramount Chiefs was of concern to their very institution. For instance, in the Southern Province of Sierra Leone, one of the oldest secondary schools in the country, named Government Secondary School Bo, or fondly known as Bo school, was established in 1906 solely to educate the sons of Paramount Chiefs.[33]

Most of the Paramount Chiefs in the country sent their sons to this school so they could emerge as future leaders of the establishment at the end of British rule. Some of them went on to inherit the thrones of their parents, and in this way, continuity was maintained. Arguably, it consolidated elitism among traditional rulers in Sierra Leone.

My father may have been a strict, astute, and unbending disciplinarian, but he was also a sociable personality. He had an excellent relationship with his siblings. Also, he accorded respect to his subjects. Hence, he was very popular and loved by them. His courtroom was considered as the crucible by his subjects, but he often enjoyed the company of his paternal brothers as well as councillors. Now and again, they would gather around him. They ate together, settled chiefdom matters together, and shared whatever he was given as the Paramount Chief.

I must reiterate that he and his siblings were very close. They agreed on virtually everything, except one. His brothers tried as best as they could to let me join their own children in a Quranic school, where nothing was taught except the Quran and Islamic ethics. His brothers wanted him to follow this suggestion because most of them were practising Muslims. Hence, they all opted to send their kids, my cousins, to Quranic schools.

You may also argue that my siblings and I were not destined for a Quranic education. While his brothers' children went to the Quranic school in our village, our father hired a private teacher from Makeni, to give me and some of my siblings private lessons in English. I still remember the name of the tutor: Karamorkoh Morray.

Initially, the private classes were conducted in a Court Barrie. With the passage of time, when the venture gained momentum and the roll increased, we became twenty-five in number. The curriculum contents were basic. At first we started with the English alphabet. After that, we progressed to word building, reading basic texts, basic spelling, nursery rhymes, and arithmetic.

When we grew in confidence, we moved one step up the learning ladder. We learned sentence structure, verb compliments of simple sentences. We were taught how to construct simple sentences. Side-by-side, at that stage, we learnt punctuation and handwriting skills.

Today, it sounds simple and like a fairy tale, but the moment the private tutor stepped his foot on our village marked the beginning of my long and rewarding journey in life.

My cousins were not the only children made to attend Quranic schools. All the other children my age in our village were Quranic pupils. My siblings and I were the lucky few, and we were the first children in our village to ever attend the Whiteman's school and gain the Whiteman's education.

I was then ten years old, five years older than the normal school going age in Western culture. My siblings who attended school with me were Sonthi, Kulokoh, Bato, and Wokle. After three years, what started as a private tuition institution conducted in a Court Barrie was transformed into a full-fledged primary school. It went down in the history of our village as the first ever school.

Quranic education and Islamic ethics and beliefs were not peculiar to Sierra Leone and our chiefdom. Before the advent of the Whiteman on our shores, with his ideas and religious beliefs, Islam and her ways of life had gained a stronghold in most of Africa. Together, my siblings and I spent a few years in the village school, taught by our village teacher that was hired from another village.

After spending a few years in our village school, in 1951, a few of my paternal brothers and I were sent to a Wesleyan primary school[34] in another village. The village is called Rogbin, six miles from our village. Pupils had to stay at this school till they reached Standard Six.

Those were exciting moments, considering the fact that it was the first time we experienced life outside the perimeters of our father's palace. Life in this village was quite different from the one we were used to at home. However, we adjusted quite well, and quickly too.

The school was within walking distance. We walked to the village on foot, attended school for half of the day, and returned home on daily basis. We made new friends, but we were given preferential treatment, being the children of a Paramount Chief, and a fearsome one at that.

I made a lot of friends in school. One of them was Jacob Kamara. I was clever in school and followed the rules to the letter. However, I needn't hide the fact that, like most children my age, I was often mischievous and naughty at school. One of my victims among the teachers was Mr Gbariyah Koroma. He was our English teacher. We used to provoke him a lot, especially with regards to his obsession with jaw-breaking words.

The following story often provoked laughter, punctuated by mockery and provocations: Teacher Koroma[35] once applied for a job in Makeni. Since he uses big words, he bombarded the application with ten—and fifteen-letter words, showing off his vocabulary. When the organisation received his application, they didn't shortlist him for an interview. According to the story, they had to use a dictionary in order to make sense of the contents of the application, due to the litany of jaw-breaking words.

The Whiteman schools were pitched here and there in some lucky villages and towns, but we lacked other social amenities. There were no motorable roads in this part of colonial Sierra Leone. Western civilisation, and the economic development that usually comes with it, was far afield during that time, especially in Temne land.

In fact, there were few local government vehicles in the entire district, let alone privately owned vehicles. Paramount Chiefs, local business tycoons, successful subsistence farmers (or not), wealth and development in the classical sense of the words were foreign concepts in thought as well as deeds.

My brothers and I used to walk six miles on foot to and from school every day, for five days a week. On our way home, we played the usual games children play. We played hide-and-seek behind the trees. We hunted birds with our catapults and chased rabbits in the bushes. We would swim in streams especially when the sun came out and was very hot, in order to quench the heat. These routines were so absorbing physically that by the time we arrived home, we were dead tired.

It was at the Wesleyan Mission Primary School in Rogbin that I started to make an impression on my father. It was a period of transformation, during which my intelligence and other capabilities came to the fore. Instinctively, I was very argumentative; I would ask critical questions, and I was always on top of my siblings in presenting a matter before the old man.

He told his paternal brothers and trusted councillors in his courtroom, "Since my son started attending the Wesleyan Mission School, I have noticed something in him. He now behaves and performs with maturity far above the level of his age."[36]

I not only made an impression on my father, I was beginning to come across as a real gem in the making. There was a hallmark of maturity and consistency in what I set out to do at school. In short, my work ethic and intelligence captured the imaginations of my teachers as well as my schoolmates.

I must state that I owe enormous gratitude to my teachers. They contributed immensely to the rich potential of my formative years. They were a very hard-working staff and unique role models to the entire school and community.

Being a Wesleyan mission school, discipline was a big part of the school's management strategy. I still remember all of our teachers, and I must emphasise that they all worked their socks off to create success out of us, their pupils. They left a lasting impression on me, to the extent I can still remember their names.

The subjects I liked most were all geared towards my future profession. I liked history, English language, English literature, Latin, and economics. We had excellent teachers for these subjects, and they taught us the prerequisites, catalysts for success. Dedication, determination, and hard work are the catalysts for success in life. I disliked mathematics, not that I didn't have the knack for it, but because of the teaching method. The teacher was very fast, to the extent that he was nicknamed "the jet flight." Whether his students understood or not, he went ahead until the end of the lesson. More often than not, most of us left the maths lesson without grasping a single addition, let alone talk of division and multiplication signs.

I must reveal that at this primary school, one phenomenon kept reoccurring, and I couldn't sweep it under the carpet. During this period of my formative years, I envisioned that I was a special case in this school.

I was not treated with contempt, but I was unique considering the fact that my father was an atheist, unlike the other pupils, whose parents were Christians. I could feel it in my soul; I felt a presence, or an on-and-off wave of intrusion. I could feel it in my psyche; I wondered if, since my dad was an atheist, the same blood ran in my veins. It could be argued that none of us has Christian, Islamic, Buddhist, or atheistic beliefs in our blood.

Whatever the reason was, I know not. But I would say that through divine inspiration, gradually, Christianity and its beliefs crept its way into my soul, the psyche of the son of an atheist, a Paramount Chief, a traditional ruler and Chief Masquerade, who had the strongest of ties with the occult world. Gradually, I underwent a unique transformation.[37]

In brief, the genes which constitute me, the entirety of my genetics, the very genes which biologically brought me into this world, may have been those of an atheist, ally of demons and mediums, but Christ and His miracles were seemingly set to sanctify those very genes of the agent of polytheism: my father.

I must confess that I was a bully, but wait a minute, even when I offended one of my brothers, and I was reported to the old man, I would invariably be the one to be appeased, because I knew how to get out of a situation, no matter how difficult. I was very good at saving my skin. Observant as my father was, he quickly realised my potential to wriggle out of any matter, even where I was the offender.

I had countless confrontations with my siblings, some serious, others minor. And each time I was brought before my dad for judgement, I won. I won not because I had a golden tongue, but because I was witty and argumentative. Hence my father always forbade me to defend myself, knowing I would win.

In one classical confrontation with one of my siblings, I knew I offended him and was guilty, hands down. But when we appeared before my father, I presented my side of the case so maturely and convincingly. All the same, my father believed in justice. He was determined to punish me for treating my sibling unfairly. He gave me some lashes with the cane.

Out of instinct, I said to my father, "This is not justice."

It was first time I had ever uttered a word against him. He was puzzled. He reacted this time not with the cane but a prophecy. It was on that day that my father predicted my future, which would later come to pass:

"You, Eddie, you are going to be the lawyer of this family. I see you as one. You shall be some kind of a leader in this country. You shall meet kings and queens and heads of states in faraway countries. You shall always be a controversial personality for it is one of the attributes, inspiration, strength, and valour of a leader. Whatever the trial and temptations, you shall never be defeated by your opponents! You shall never lose any battle. You shall always be a step ahead of your enemies, and defeat any obstacle that comes your way."[38.]

My formative years took shape nicely. In 1954, I attended the Church of England Primary School[39] in Makeni (a metropolitan city in the Northern Province) to do my Standard Six after my time at the Wesleyan Mission School. Amazingly, I spent only one day at the school before quitting, due to their draconian methods of administering discipline. Unreasonably, their heavy-handedness was shrouded in so-called stringent school rules and discipline. My father didn't dispute my misgivings about the school; he supported my action.

After that, I transferred to Our Lady of Fatima Primary School in Makeni. Unlike my former school, Our Lady of Fatima is a

Roman Catholic school.[40] I underwent a second phase of religious transformation. The Catholic mission is committed to spreading the Catholic faith through their schools and the church.

At Our Lady of Fatima, we memorised and recited the Lord's Prayer, Hail Mary, and the Apostle's Creed. These prayers were said at devotions and before we went home at the end of each school day. My stay at Our Lady of Fatima was important because it was there that I sat to the Common Entrance examinations, which matriculated me for secondary school.

Also, it was at this school that I was baptised to become a full-fledged Roman Catholic. It was a religious transformation in my life. The person who effectuated that transformation was Revered Father Osylivan, an Irish Catholic priest. Our Lady of Fatima Primary School was a feeder school for secondary schools in the district.

However, some parents let their children attend other secondary schools outside the district. I was one of them. In 1956, after successfully passing the Common Entrance examinations at Our Lady of Fatima, I was admitted to the St Edwards Secondary School, Freetown, on a government scholarship. My academic performance had paid great dividends. It was a big leap because, for the first time, I had to leave our district and region. At St Edwards, life was a different kettle of fish.

I had turned eighteen, and my experience, maturity, and realisation were shaping nicely, often bordering on acute sensitivity. I was very much conscious about anything happening around me. St Edwards Secondary is the pride of the Catholic mission in Sierra Leone. The school encouraged sportsmanship and high academic standards. Stoic disciplinary measures were taken against dissent.

The school was divided into three main streams. There were two classes of Form One (Form 1.1 for eleven-year-olds and Form 1.2 for fourteen—and fifteen-year-olds), and a notorious stream known as "Form One Removed," which comprised mostly older boys who entered secondary school very late and had gaps in their academic performance.[41]

In those days, our principals were Catholic priests. They were mostly Irish priests, very pious, astute, intelligent, and strict to the letter. I still remember the names of our priests: Reverend Father Martin and Father Mackie. The latter became a principal and continued the fruitful policies of his predecessors, which inspired success.

St Edwards's success rates became the envy of the other schools. Our quality was phenomenal. The school was every parent's first choice. The passing rate increased considerably, and graduates went on to enter higher educational institutions, including the University of Sierra Leone's Fourah Bay College (FBC). Others went abroad for further studies or were absorbed into the civil service, Armed Forces, or other walks of life. Overall, we did the school, the township, our parents, and the country proud, whether in the workplace or in educational institutions.

Punishment for breaking school rules ranged from kneeling down in front of the class to being sent to a corner of the room. Culprits were also made to copy an entire textbook of about two hundred pages. One of my schoolmates at St Edwards was Stephen Bio, one of Sierra Leone's most successful football stars.

You can appreciate that going to St Edwards in Freetown did present a different cultural experience to this provincial boy. In addition to the intermittent cultural shocks, there were also the periodic waves of nostalgia and homesickness. Social life in the metropolis of Freetown was fast, complex, and sometimes misleading. Our country was preparing for the challenges as well as opportunities of the post-colonial era. There were anxieties that we would add to crème of those destined to inherit the new age. Yes, those were exciting times full of sweet dreams, but all of these dreams came with hard work, seriousness, and self-belief.

I had a firm footing on the soil of Freetown and St Edwards. Everything was going very well for me, but then the worst happened.

It was the last straw that broke the camel's back. My father died in 1953. His death had a debilitating impact on me.

My father was everything to me. He was my unfailing friend, my trusted and benevolent mentor, my role model, and my motivator. Our only point of divergence was our different religious beliefs. Amazingly, while the Great Man was an atheist, he allowed me the freedom of worship, a freedom most atheists do not allow their loved ones. He gave me his fatherly blessings and allowed me to convert to Christianity. That phenomenon made my father a paradox to his subjects, his siblings, and most other people. On one hand, he believed in demons and communicated with mediums, yet he let his children have the freedom to become Christians.

The year 1961 was pivotal in my formative development. I completed my schooling at St Edwards Secondary School and passed my "O" level examinations. It also coincided with two historical events in the history of our country. On 27 April 1961, Sierra Leone was granted self-rule, with the right to take care of her own destiny. Secondly, this awesome occasion was graced by a visit from Her Majesty, Queen Elizabeth II. Though I was a student at the St Edwards Secondary School in Freetown, I rushed to Makeni, when the Queen extended her royal visit as part of the nationwide celebrations of independence.[42]

Children clad in their immaculate school uniforms and all the chieftains converged on Makeni Township, waving the green, white, and blue flag of our newly independent Sierra Leone. United in body and spirit, we all waved as we marched to the melodious tunes of schools bands playing songs and native music. The pomp and pageantry were magnificent. The entire population in this part of the country responded to this national call, because it was once-in-a-lifetime opportunity.

Primary and secondary school pupils, teachers, Paramount Chiefs, chiefdom elders, and tribal authorities descended on Makeni. We lined up along the routes to Wusum Field. We clapped in unison as we chanted jubilantly, "God save the Queen, God save the Queen." That day went down in the annals of the history of Makeni (and our country at large). I was blessed and proud to be part of that awesome occasion.

The young Queen was splendid in her royal attire and regalia. She was very pretty and radiant, in my youthful eyes. Little did I know, I would meet her face to face, later in my career as a diplomat.

Indeed, little did I know that I would one day present my credentials to her, this time in my capacity as Sierra Leone's High Commissioner to the Court of St. James in London.

After secondary education, the realities of my new life dawned on me. In fact, for some harrowing time, they lingered. No father, no mother, and no half brothers or sisters weighed heavily on my teenage mind and thinking. I was alone, desperate, and unhappy. Many unfamiliar questions surged unbearably, to the extent that I sometimes couldn't cope with them. I couldn't answer them. All I did more often than not was ponder into the abyss. Many questions, and few or no answers at all, blighted this period in my life.

After the solitude, one plan sprang to my mind. A job! Of course, I needed a job. Fortunately, I was hired after my first attempt. The Barclays Bank DCO posted me to a sub-branch in Lunsar. At that time, Lunsar was a bustling, medium-sized town with a huge percentage of mine workers. I have to stress that I was very fortunate to meet a lot of people with whom I cultivated friendships, and among them was President Siaka Stevens, a brilliant trade unionist. I had a splendid time working at Barclays. I was with them from 1962 to early 1968.

It is customary for natives and provincials to marry early and raise a family. In some families, there is no compromise; it is incumbent on the offspring to do so, or else they suffer the wrath of their parents and extended families. The rationale is that a household without a child is one without respectability and dignity. In the typical African culture, a man's clout and pedigree are judged by whether he has a wife or not. Men attain positions of trust among their kinsmen only if they are married with children. There is a lot at stake in being married and having children at an early age.

Now and again, women are under pressure if they fail to bear a child, children in their matrimonial homes. "You must bear my son a child," mothers often warned the wives of their children. "We can't encourage a barren wife in this family."

During my years in Sierra Leone, I had two children with Laura Aubee; they are all grown up and live independent lives now. Hawa Turay resides in London, and her brother Sallieu Turay is an inspiring story, worth emulating by others. He went through primary and secondary school and gained impressive "O" and "A" levels, but then he fell short of pursuing a degree.

It was disheartening to the family.

One day I sat him down and admonished him:

"You have a choice, you must enter university, and get a degree like your other siblings, or remain an undergraduate and become the proverbial gate keeper for them in the future, because they have gained higher qualifications."

As the Lord would have it, he heeded my advice; at the age of forty-one, he entered Fourah Bay College and eventually got a degree. He is in the process of coming to England in order to pursue his postgraduate studies.

I had another relationship with Princess Jah from Moyamba. She bore me three lovely children: Joy (now Mrs Joy Brown), who has an MA degree, Eddie Boy, and Prince Turay. The latter is a graduate of FBC. After my relationship with Princess Jah, my next partner was Mary Sellu (now deceased). We had a son named Orbai Turay, who has decided to take after me by reading law at FBC. Sadly, our second child, Haja Turay, died in a plane accident.

All the time I worked at Barclays in Sierra Leone, I set my eyes on one dream: to venture abroad, study, and improve myself academically. I had always held tight to the belief that with quality skills and qualifications, anything is possible. I also realised that qualifications and skills were being sought after by most of Africa's former colonies, to the extent that some of their home-grown graduates were being ignored for overseas graduates. Graduates from the United Kingdom were treated as the real jewels in the crown. Even young beautiful girls prayed for graduates from the UK to be their suitors.

Of course, there were other options on the cards. Opportunities came my way to migrate to the United States or Canada, but the United Kingdom was my choice. And to this day, I don't regret my choice.

However, there is always a premonition, fear, or phobia of travelling. Travelling out of one's country into an unfamiliar territory is similar to venturing into the unknown. Also, I could have continued to serve at Barclays Bank, climb the ladder, make money, and then opt for an early political career.

But I had one concrete idea in my mind: study abroad. Luckily, I had one thing on my side. It is that priceless thing, grace, they call faith. My religious upbringing coupled with the prophecies of my late father had emboldened me. It was decision time! Eventually, I resigned my job at the Barclays Bank in order to venture into the unknown.

CHAPTER 3

A JOURNEY TO THE UNKNOWN

———◦———

"It is of essence that mankind experiments with the unknown sometimes. It could count after all as a blessing in disguise. Life is a risk; those who take the risk more often than not reap the benefits."

The Philosophy of the Adventurers of the Old

As I read the quotation above now and reflect on the benefits I have reaped (and continue to reap) because of the risks I took then, I have faith in this philosophy and admonish others to do the same. Don't be scared; take a measured, reasonable risk in your life.

Don't sit idly and wait for fortune and opportunity to smile at you. Don't say it will come looking for you. That is wishful thinking, and it bears no good fruits. Remember, life was not created on the premise of wishful thinking. Go, venture out, and seek for fortunes and opportunities, for there are too many competitors out there, and each one of them is more anxious and hungrier for it than you, the wishful thinker.

However, whatever adventure you embark on, I admonish you to take calculated risks and analyse the advantages and disadvantages before you make a move. In other words, don't leap into the dark, the abyss, unless you at least have a slight knowledge of the terrain.

Late in 1968, I ventured into the unknown. I left Sierra Leone for the UK, sailing on the last voyage of the Steamship *Apapa* of Cunard Lines.[43] This was a great moment for me and an incredible experience. I was afraid as the huge ocean waves battered the ship. Though this vessel was massive, the ocean waves rocked it to the discomfort of every crew member on board. The journey took almost two weeks; the ship sailed from Ghana, Nigeria, Sierra Leone, and Gambia and onwards to Liverpool in the UK.

Historically speaking, the late 1950s and 1960s were decades of adventurism. There was a massive surge in the ambitions of young people to migrate abroad and search for greener pastures. This was the impact of the wider ramifications of the very much talked about "Wind of Change," heralded in British Prime Minister Harold Macmillan's famous speech. British colonialism had come to its end.[44]

The Wind of Change brought in its wake a unique historical era of emancipation. In 1957, Ghana gained her independence under Dr Kwame Nkrumah (of the "Africa for the African" philosophy). Nigeria became independent in 1960, and then my country, Sierra Leone, in 1961, followed by Gambia four years later. These were exciting moments. However, as the saying goes, autonomy comes with a price.

You would appreciate that at the departure of the colonial masters and their expatriate staff, who'd manned the public services throughout colonialism, Africa was short of people with the needed skills and expertise. Political autonomy was undoubtedly required, for it was priceless; it left a huge vacuum to be filed.

The continent needed qualified personnel to fill in the gaps in the key areas: education, trade and commerce, engineering, the judiciary, health service, civil service, the police, and the armed forces. Since these skills were not available in the newly independent countries, young people decided to travel to their former motherland, the UK, in order to acquire them.

On board the ship, there were hundreds of youngsters from West Africa. There were migrants from Nigeria, Ghana (formally the Gold Coast), Gambia, and Sierra Leone. We arrived in Liverpool early in the morning. Our first experience was a terribly cold winter day.

Due to our ignorance of the weather in the UK, none of us youngsters had prepared for this kind of terrible weather. Back in our various countries, we basked in the glorious sunshine for six months, and there is nothing like winter. Hence, none of us had winter clothing, including winter coats or heavy clothes, to brave the harsh weather. The freezing cold pierced through our bones, as we stood there, shivering like leaves on trees.

For me, there was a much more difficult problem at hand: my host and compatriot, one Mr Victor Johnson, who was supposed to meet me at the dockyards, did not turn up at all. I was stranded in no man's land.

I was shocked, as we were best of friends back in Sierra Leone when he worked for the Barclays Bank. Victor was not only my friend and workmate, he was one of my few bosom friends. Hence, when he invited me to join him in the United Kingdom, there was no need to be apprehensive, let alone talk of any doubt.

I was torn apart, completely in a state of limbo. One could just imagine the sense of loss and distress I found myself in Liverpool, there on my first day in the UK. All my original strategies, plans, hopes of having the opportunity to graze like a lucky sheep on fertile, greener pastures of England appeared shattered.

This brings me back to the prophecy of my late father. As I waited in vain, I said a little prayer in silence. I prayed, "Lord, you spoke through my dad since I was born, that my destiny is abroad, and nowhere else. You told him to tell me that I shall one day dine with the Great and the Good. If his prophesy meant anything as revealed to him, Lord, I sincerely do believe that come what may, you will work a miracle right now in my life. My Good Lord and Saviour, come to my rescue at this crucial moment in this foreign land, I beseech you!"[45]

I want to believe that while I was praying, a divine voice must have exclaimed in laughter, "Oh ye mortals of little faith, why doubt my divine grace and intervention, for those I favour!"

And it was indeed the case. For even before I stood there, stranded in the freezing winter in no man's land, praying for a miracle, divine provisions had been made for my arrival, in case I was caught up in any manner of difficulty.

It was indeed a miracle I shall never forget. This was how it happened. I had travelled on the boat with a young lady, who I later came to know as Mrs Kpakewa, a Sierra Leonean national. It was my destined rescuer's first time to England. But there was a difference between her situation and mine.

I was left stranded due to a failing promise by my would-be host. She, on the other hand, was coming to join her husband, though for the first time. In fact, it was later revealed to me that she came after their proxy wedding in Sierra Leone.

What actually emboldened me to take the step, the undoubtedly giant leap I took, remains a miracle to this day. I took another leap of faith, and luckily, the jigsaw pieces fell into place. I approached this young lady and pleaded with her to take me wherever her husband took her. When Mr Kpakewa arrived to pick her up, she entreated with him to assist me. And to my amazed delight, her husband agreed with genuine pleasure.

The husband lived in Manchester, in northwest England. These Good Samaritans literary took me under their wings. Eventually, out of miracles, the son of man was offered a place to lay his head.

We arrived in Manchester late in the day. No need to shout and be excited just yet. Just hang on a moment; on arrival at my hosts' apartment, I noticed that there was only one bedroom. My face fell; I was dispirited and consumed by renewed gloom.

In my hearts of hearts, I felt so bad for creating an inconvenience for the couple during their very first night together. Intruding on their nuptial bliss bothered me throughout the night. I had to endure a sleepless night as I kept muttering, "Oh dear, what an embarrassment, what an inconvenience to this poor couple."

When I look upon that particular night and the subsequent hospitality the couple lavished on me, I continue to pray for them and their families wherever they may be. In all honesty, to say that they were generous and caring human beings would be an understatement. Because they put up with this inconvenience: we all slept in the same room—the couple in the bed, and I, on the settee. If anything, I felt so guilty for being a nuisance that night to the couple.

Life in a foreign land permits no time wasting, no premonitions, and no postponement of whatever idea comes your way. The best thing to do is to put it to the test and see what becomes of it. Now that I had landed and had an abode, a place to lay my head, it was worth taking further risks. But again, always remember, it must be a calculated risk.

Mind you, don't ever doubt yourself. Always keep the faith. There is always a second chance, as long as it is a calculated risk. You have to think on your feet, so the next day, I pleaded with the husband to get me a job as soon as possible. As further testament to their humanity, he agreed and got me a cleaning job at the Grand Hotel in Piccadilly in Manchester.

In those days, there were many jobs, especially menial jobs for migrants, in the industrialised parts of the UK. There were manufacturing and building companies, retail businesses, and offices to clean. Historically, Manchester has always enjoyed a rich economy in the UK. It had rich immigrant communities, especially Africans and Caribbeans. The latter group were known in those days as West Indians.

A cleaning job was not necessarily my choice, being a lowly paid job, and besides, there is a demeaning stigma that hangs over all menial jobs. However, be cautious; don't read too much into this. The fact is that the name of the game is simply survival. When in Rome, do as the Romans: invest, trust in situational ethics, and get on with life no matter the condition.

History teaches us that migration has been a contentious matter since time immemorial. No matter how rich a country may be, there will always be a scarcity of resources. Therefore, due to this scarcity, the redistribution of wealth, compounded by entrenched elitism, there is always going to be a backlash against people who migrate from poorer or less developed countries to richer ones, looking for greener pastures.

It is not peculiar to the UK or any other country in the world. In fact, globalisation and post-modernism have combined to make a global village where migration, political contact, and socio-economic interaction are naturally actuated. It is not a matter of choice any more; despite the barricades, people will move backwards and forwards. Also, what has not been talked about by the media, political commentators, and politicians is that people have different reasons for their movements from their homelands to foreign countries.

Hence, generally speaking, the United Kingdom in the sixties and seventies was relatively receptive to migrants, considering the prevailing political climate. For instance, just three days after my arrival, my friend secured me my first job in the UK.

Looking at the bigger picture, it could be argued that racial discrimination did happen, not necessarily by design but default. The post-WWII period took its tolls on social investment and the redistribution of wealth.

There were always tensions, and in more cases than not, migrants were at the receiving end: the innocent, unfortunate victims. Reflecting once more on the intervention of the divine and the luck that came with it for me, I must confess that I didn't encounter any form of racism. In fact, the very day that my host applied for a job on my behalf, I had the offer.

The pay was not necessarily fantastic, but given the circumstances, it was handsome for me. It was enough to pay my rent and finance my food and other basic needs. The first room I rented for myself was on Hathersage Road, and I moved just three days after my arrival in the UK.

I enjoyed my cleaning job, because it suited my other interests. It was a night job, and my duties included cleaning the kitchen. And the big advantage was that food was provided for me in the evening, and I had a good breakfast when I clocked out early in the morning. Being single, young, and void of extra financial costs to meet, this job was suitable for me. I was excited by my new "opportunity."

It seemed I had settled down, so I continued with my cleaning job, absolutely oblivious of anything else in the world. Having said that, my new opportunity on arrival did not blind me to the realities of my migration to the United Kingdom. Yes, I had settled in nicely, with a job, a roof over my head, a sense of financial security, and the hope to dream, dream, and dream beyond my wildest dreams. That dream and the routes that were taken to accomplish it constitute my next chapter.

CHAPTER 4

URGE FOR FURTHER EDUCATION

⟨⊙⟩

"Some would argue that the zest to advance your dreams further sometimes requires the perfect cushions. For me it sounds like the philosophy of weak, the feeble. It is those who lack self-belief. For all dreams have to be sought after, through blood and sweat."

Dreamland and Its Revealing Tricks,
**South London Private Armature Theatre Scripts,
2012 Series**

There is a story behind every success, and more often than not, the story is not linear. The route is not always smooth, but rough and tempting. There are those who meander their way. Others stumble and fall and write themselves out of the race to the finish. What I am trying to state is that the textual genesis of success is complex.

It is in this context that I said:

"Those who seek success must be prepared to consume dirt; they must be prepared to starve. Ceaselessly, they must wallow in the unknown until it is assured, beyond all reasonable doubts, they are there, and then they can claim success."

Therefore, since success rarely comes to the meek and feeble; it is priceless. It is the reason why we should sacrifice all we can in order to attain success. Wallowing in the mucky waters to seek success, I always had one thing at the back of my mind. I knew that education — real and functional education — was the only catalyst for all I hoped to achieve in life. That thing was education, and a solid one at that. I worked for approximately two years as a cleaner at the hotel.

As I said before, I was enjoying my job and the flexible hours. That alone was an opportunity in itself for me to polish my dream and advance it further. I knew that it would be inconceivable to wait for a cushion. Wait for a cushion! Who would offer me one, if any at all? I was an orphan, and above all, I was a sojourner in a foreign land, picking the breadcrumbs at the table in order to survive.

In totality, there was only one way out; I mentioned it before and emphasise it once more because of its significance. Education was the only answer to my quest to achieve my father's dream. His prophesy would only make sense if I gained an education and pursued the law career he had confidently predicted, and fulfil the prophesy well before he joined his ancestors.

I was now in the hub, the very theatre where dreams were made through education and qualifications. British qualifications were (and are still) admired everywhere in the world. It is one of the reasons why the world migrates to this small but academically advanced island. It was as a result of her prowess in education that Britannia ruled the waves and dominated three-quarters of the world as a superior empire.

My first concrete step to attain my dream was enrolling at the St. John's College of Further Education. I studied for a banking diploma at the Institute of Bankers of England and Wales. I would have loved to study full time, but I was constrained by the demands of my cleaning job at the Grand Hotel. I had no choice but opt for a part-time course. Hence, I was able to kill two birds with one stone. I was comfortable with the academic demands of the course, having had a good pedigree in Sierra Leone.

In 1972, events took a different dimension in my life. While I was still reading for the diploma in banking, I came across an advertisement in the *Evening Standard* in Manchester. It was fascinating; I weighed the prospects and realised that they would put me in good stead to become a lawyer. The New Manchester Polytechnic (now Metropolitan University) sought applications from the public for admission to the school.

It was the period of the polytechnic, a two-tiered system of education in England and Wales. I need to go a bit into the history of this educational institution. They were not a second grade university or a tertiary institution, as often perceived by some critics. They were tertiary education teaching institutions in England, Wales, and Northern Ireland.

The courses they offered varied, but they were like technological universities in other countries; their aim was to teach both purely academic and professional vocational subjects. Their focus was applied education for work, and they concentrated on engineering and applied science (though soon after being founded, they also created humanities departments).

They offered undergraduate and postgraduate degrees that were administered at the national level. In 1992, the Further Education Act transformed polytechnics into independent universities, which meant they were authorised to award their own degrees.

Prior to the 1992 act, they awarded degrees under the auspices of mainstream universities. Notwithstanding that, their degrees were still accredited and solid. Also, their accreditation system was equally as vigorous as the mainstream universities.

While most polytechnics were formed in the expansion of higher education in the 1960s, some can trace their history back much further than this. For instance, the London Polytechnic, which is now the

University of Westminster, emerged from the Royal Polytechnic Institution, which was founded in 1838. The establishment of the polytechnic was a reaction to the rise of industrial power and technical education in France.[46]

Whatever the perception about polytechnics, there is an old adage that says, "It is not the coat that matters, but the man in the coat." I immediately applied for and secured a place to read law. Truly, I was just a whisker from my long dream and that of my late father. Remember, when he was alive, he always referred to my argumentative character as the ultimate gift for a future lawyer.

I have to say, though, that law is not just about being argumentative. He didn't realise this salient point. You need an analytical brain, to think critically and be alert. You also need to undergo academic training in writing skills at the highest level. You need to be tuned to informed judgement. A lawyer can't afford to reach judgement just for novelty sake or through sentiments. The logical conclusions, which inform the judgements a lawyer reaches, is of the essence.

Would anyone blame my dad for having a simplistic and contrary view about law? No, in my opinion, I don't think so. In retrospect, who would ever blame him? Not even as he rests in peace with his ancestors. He wasn't an educated man, so assessing the in-depth rigors of this discipline that has gained universal acclaim as the toughest would be an unfair judgement, to say the least.

Another phase of luck struck. The Manchester City Corporation offered me a grant to cover the costs of the course. It was rare, given the challenges which often stand in the way of foreign students. I did justice to myself and to those who put their trust in me by awarding me the grant, the Manchester City Corporation. Above all, I did make the spirits of my late parents proud, as well as my country and myself. I studied very hard and proved my mettle.

More often than not, academic challenges are not of plain sailing. At first, as natural as these things can be, doubts crept in intermittently. But I weathered the storm and took my studies seriously. This was good and divine. I met every deadline, presented every essay on time, did every presentation, went to every seminar, sat to all my examinations, and met every criterion meticulously.

In 1975, I graduated with honours. There was one more phase left. Graduating with an academic degree does not qualify you to practice law. Without wasting any time, in the same year, I engaged the final phase of my long journey. I enrolled at the Inns of Court School of Law and graduated in 1976.[47]

It was time to be rightly accorded the accolade I deserved after years of hard work, years of aspiring to attain my dream. I must make mention of one particular lecturer who motivated me: Raymond, the head of the Law Department. His message was simple—work hard, burn the candle at both ends, and you will become a lawyer.

I was called to the bar at Lincoln's Inn in 1976. I was amazed at the magnitude of my strides. They constitute the perfect characteristics of the classic quantum leap. On reflection, I thought about how my late father had predicted I would become a lawyer. As I held my results in my hand, fully clad in my academic gown, tears ran down my cheeks. They were unique tears, tears of joy and sorrow.

In addition to my studies, I also enjoyed a fruitful social life. My first partner in England was a West Indian lady named Lorna. We had three children—Mariatu Turay (an analyst with the British government with an MA degree), Michael Turay (an IT specialist, aspiring to become a pastor), and Edwin Turay, who is serving in the British Army.

When I reflect on my catalogue of achievements, I must state that I walk with my shoulders high. On the other hand, I shed those tears stated inter alia, as symbols of pity for my late father. My benevolent dad had made the forecast; he inspired and motivated me to read the law, which I finally gained with honours.

Thanks be to God and my father, I had been called to the bar and qualified as a practicing lawyer from one of the renowned inns in the world. With the law degree and the right to practice as a lawyer, I confirmed in my mind the conduit through which my father's prophesies would come to pass in my life. As always, I offered prayers for His Grace's goodness to me and the memory of my dad.

Throughout my years away from Sierra Leone, I kept in touch with family and friends. They say a leopard never changes its sports. I am the son of a Paramount Chief, a traditional ruler. It was a reality I always had in my sub-consciousness, no matter what I did. Most significantly, I am a patriotic nationalist to the core, so my native land, Sierra Leone, and the imperative on my shoulders to make it proud, remained part and parcel of my entire dream whilst abroad.

I had completed my law degree, was called to the bar, and had the world of opportunities at my beck and call. Little did I know that another wave of migration would knock on my door. It came like a thief in the night, when I least expected. After my call to the bar in England, I was offered a legal position by the government of Jamaica, which I quickly accepted.

Most of my friends and compatriots, at home and abroad, were cautious. They posed many salient questions:

"Why on earth would you choose to go to Jamaica? Why can't you try your luck in the UK, especially since you qualified here?"

They were spot on, considering the fact that there were not many black lawyers in the UK. Had I tried my luck, I would have had the chance to practice in England. However, Jamaica was not a misplaced choice. Like Sierra Leone, it was a former British colony and practiced the same law as in England.

Also, my immediate acceptance was motivated by a determination to arm myself with all the necessary skills and experience in my profession. I knew it would prepare me for a glorious return to my country. I envisioned that my choice to work in Jamaica wasn't wasted. It would present me with invaluable opportunities.

Challenges! Of course, there are challenges in all we choose to do in life. I was prepared for them, and I knew there would be enormous challenges ahead in Jamaica. The advantages associated with these challenges, I reckoned, would prepare me for bigger things ahead at home or elsewhere in Africa, where lawyers were in high demand.

CHAPTER 5

MIGRATION TO JAMAICA

—◦○◦—

"Experience is the best teacher, especially that which
you acquire in another terrain. It is invaluable because
it is not a textbook culture, practice, or theoretical
tuition. More often than not one learns it the hard way.
Whichever way it is experienced, it is of hard core and
extremely invaluable."

Venturing Abroad: The Hub Stories

The saying goes that life is sometimes unpredictable. And in my case,
this is akin to the gospel truth. My next port of call didn't come about
as a result of any form of preplanning by me. No one planned it, other
than my divine agent, who guides and directs my life. Following the
other significant divine happenings, which brought me to this point,
I subsequently crossed the Atlantic, first to the UK and then the
Caribbean, known in those days as the West Indies.

Historically, my race had travelled to these shores not out of their own
volition but through force. It was imposed on them. Amidst inhuman
conditions, blacks from all over Africa were put in chains and shipped

53

across the Atlantic Ocean to England, the West Indies, and the Americas. This was dubbed the trans-Atlantic slave trade.[48]

It is a sad history, but it is worth narrating here because of its historical significance, and its triangular significance which relates to me and my race.

First, there were millions of freed slaves who were repatriated to these islands of West Indies, from all over Africa. They came from my country, Sierra Leone, and my regional neighbours, including Nigeria, Ghana, Gambia, and Senegal, to name a handful.

The second point is even more poignant. We are one and the same racially and culturally. We share the same history, and our forefathers, the victims of slavery, were common victims. Unfortunately, it was only the trans-Atlantic slave trade and colonialism that separated us, but the settlers of these islands and most Africans share similar cultures and beliefs.

Third, that we are so divided, even in post-modern times, is due to the fact that the divide and rule colonial strategy actually worked on our psyches. It is sad to reflect that the first generation of our brothers and sisters landed on these shores after they were forcefully removed from the rest of their kindred. This forced removal constitutes one of the main reasons why Caribbeans and Africans think they are different from each other.

It is sad to say, and I say this not out of arrogance or empty pride, but through humility, I was destined to arrive in grand style in the Caribbean, as an officer of the government of a country of descendants of freed slaves. It happened in this way. Early in 1976, I joined the Jamaican judiciary as deputy clerk of courts. I was posted to Montego Bay as deputy clerk of courts for a year and then promoted to the position of clerk of courts.[49]

Jamaica was (and is still) a beautiful country. I was at home with the country, and in hindsight, it was obviously natural. The Jamaicans have the same features as Sierra Leoneans, a mixture of dark skin and half-cast or fair skin. Like in Sierra Leone and elsewhere in Africa, there are people of mixed race, borne out of cross-cultural marriages.

The country has a rich, strong, and vibrant culture. On the surface it seems to be homogeneous, but the actually is that it is heterogeneous. The Creoles of Sierra Leone share some cultures and traditions with Jamaicans, including Christianity. There are more churches in Jamaica than anywhere in Africa.

Similarly, in the metropolitan city of Freetown, the seat of government and home to the Creoles, the number of churches is amazing. Some Jamaicans celebrate a loved one's death with a nine-day wake; similar customs of wake keeping exist in Sierra Leone.

During the time I was in Jamaica, the prime minister was Michael Manley. He was Jamaica's third prime minister. He was a member of the People's National Party. He was PM from March 1972 to November 1980. He returned to be prime minister for a second time from February 1989 to March 1992.[50]

Michael Manley was a very popular leader, and he wielded immense power. But there were concerns about the wave of crime in the country. Like his predecessors, he was not able to get a grip on crime. During my period in Jamaica, the crime wave was notorious.

The country was engulfed in extreme violence, notably against women. As one would expect, I was assigned the most grotesque cases to prosecute. The reason was simple: Jamaican prosecutors (or their families) sometimes faced reprisals for handling cases involving violent criminals.

I was special in the sense that I was considered a safe pair of hands. The criminals had no axe to grind with me as a foreign national. The reason is obvious. In addition to the fact that I am not a Jamaican, I had no relations in Jamaica. I was alone and had no family members to be concerned about, as I had none in Jamaica at the time.

I executed my duties judiciously and made an immediate impression on my bosses as well as my colleagues and most of the islanders. Most island settlements are social hubs. Jamaica is no exception. The island is frequented by tens of thousands of tourists throughout the year.

I really enjoyed my time in Jamaica; I made a lot of friends, so despite the wave of criminality and the impact on the judiciary, I remained in love with the country. Again, at last, divine providence lifted me out of Jamaica when I least expected.

The architect was Sierra Leone's longest serving president, Siaka Stevens. In 1978, the president paid a visit to Jamaica. According to protocol, a group of Sierra Leonean residents in Jamaica, including myself, paid a courtesy call to his hotel. He received us well and pleaded with us to return home to assist in the development of our country. One of his regime's strategic policies was to recruit Sierra Leoneans in the diaspora to return to participate in the politics of their homeland.[51]

It was a very good strategy; the president appealed to educated and qualified diasporas to return home and participate in nation building. And many of those who returned were absorbed into mainstream politics, the judiciary, the commercial sector, the civil service, the police force, the prison service, and the Sierra Leone Army.

The meeting with Stevens was conducted informally. We were introduced to him in turns. When it was my turn, he took an interest in my mission in Jamaica. As a strategist and pragmatist, the president decided to lure me into returning home. They say there is no place like home. I took the bait, at least in principle, because I was still in two minds. The president promised to get me a job in the Judicial Department.

I was constrained to disappoint the president. That same year, 1978, I returned to London. Luckily, I secured a job as a clerical assistant and worked for a year with the Inland Revenue Authority in Manchester. This tax district was responsible for taxpayers in the London area.

It was a great experience working with white folks in a group, instead of working alone in a kitchen, as during my previous job. They were helpful and friendly at that work place, but they had a particular habit that was unfriendly. As soon as we parted company, after work, they would lose memory of me completely. Even if we both happened to cross the same pedestrian crossing point, they acted as if they had never seen me in their life.

At the Inland Revue, it was quite the opposite. I enjoyed the office and much more refined culture and practices. I must reveal that I was beginning to get my feet on the ground. I never thought I would contemplate leaving this job. All the same, I had no choice, and eventually I did leave.

CHAPTER 6

THE CALL TO RETURN HOME

⌐○⌐

"There is nothing more fitting and honourable than to serve your fellowman and country. For service to others, as service to thyself, is sweet, refreshing, productive, and more rewording."

Dr Martin Luther King Jr.
(paraphrased; 1929-1968))

In the previous chapter, I mentioned that President Stevens promised that when I returned home, I could join the Justice Department of Sierra Leone. True to His Excellency's promise, he confirmed this when he returned home after his official tour of Jamaica. Initially, I was tempted to decide otherwise. But according to Lorna Arthur (2006), "When under pressure or faced with crucial decisions to make, be steadfast. Temptation is fuelled by emotion not logic, so use positive emotions to combat it."

My departure coincided with the victory of Margaret Thatcher and her Conservative Party in the polls. On 1 May 1979, I cast my last vote in the UK, after which I rushed to the airport to return home to Sierra Leone, to Africa. As I looked around and took in the skies, the airspace, and the beautiful terrain of what had been my safe haven for many years, I went through many emotions. Tears ran down my cheeks as I prayed for peace and prosperity to flourish in Great Britain.

I did this naturally, out of gratitude. We may talk all night long about the contentious arguments of colonialism. But there was an undisputable truism, for which we must not be ashamed to pay gratitude. Those of us who were lucky to migrate to this popular country, the historic UK, in order to improve our lot, owe a lot to this country. We must always be grateful for the opportunities we achieved in this country. There is a saying by a prolific African writer: "Those whose nuts are cracked by benevolent spirits must not forget to be humble."

As you can imagine, it was the most crucial and difficult decision I had to make in my life. I was turned between paying heed to the call to serve my country, and staying put in the UK and utilising the opportunities at my disposal. I chose the former, which I did genuinely, in the spirit of patriotism.

The logical analysis: During that crucial moment in 1979, I pondered on the logic which informed the decision I was about to make. The United Kingdom has a huge amount of manpower, covering all walks of life. In other words, the UK (and most industrialised countries in the world) are self-sufficient in terms of social capital. Sierra Leone and other developing (or third world) countries had just assumed political independence and were struggling to fill in the vacuum in various keys skills and professions.

I thought very hard, pondered on the critical issue at hand, and said these words slowly and quietly as if I was soliloquising:

"Eddie Turay, the son of late Paramount Chief Kande Turay, go home to your countrymen. You can't afford to add to the column of brain drains, so go home and be of immense service to your country, Sierra Leone. You can still go to Sierra Leone and remain loyal and grateful to the UK."

Secondly, in my heart of hearts, I knew my dead father's spirits must have prevailed on me to make the decision. He was a nationalist and a true patriot, values he never compromised throughout his life. So, without a shadow of doubt, he wouldn't have decided otherwise.

When I finally landed in my country, I was appointed resident magistrate for Moyamba and Bonthe Districts, with residence in Moyamba town. These districts are in the Southern Province of Sierra Leone.

I was very much excited at my new role. It was a great honour bestowed on me by the government and judiciary of my country. I had acquired all the necessary skills, qualifications, and invaluable experiences in Jamaica. On top of that, I was very young and had the prospects of a huge and bright future ahead of me in my profession. By the time I returned home and took up this appointment, Sierra Leone had just passed eight years as a post-colonial state.

Obviously, there were enormous challenges all Sierra Leoneans, from various walks of life, had to deal with. The watchwords that would galvanise us all as a nation and embrace this course were togetherness and national unity and discipline in our attitudes and character towards one another, our local communities, and above all the state. We were (and are still) required to bury our regional, ethnic, or call it tribal differences and obey that which holds us together as one inseparable unit: the laws of the land borne out of the constitution written by us as a nation.

I was a young, dynamic, qualified barrister from the United Kingdom. However, I was not adequately prepared for certain things. I say this not as a result of fear or incompetence on my part, but because some of the issues, the concrete challenges I experienced, were not textbook matters or theories.

One of these imposingly formidable challenges was how people reacted to the implementation of the law. Sierra Leone didn't have a lot of violent crime, but criminality was everywhere, geopolitical differences notwithstanding. The second challenge was that eight years as an independent nation had been marked by dramatic changes, including passing the political baton from one political party to another (sometimes punctuated by intermittent military coup attempts to disrupt the young democratic process that was about to blossom).

Especially in the local population, there were some unscrupulous elements in the population who took chances with the laws of the land. And the sad thing was that they did this at the expense of political stability and national cohesiveness.

What they didn't realise was that they were dealing with a different kettle of fish. My love and respect for the law of the land knows no bounds. Hence, whoever abuses the law would definitely find himself at odds with me. These recalcitrant abusers of the law and authority had misjudged me completely.

They thought they could take the law into their hands, because they were officials or were affiliated with the ruling party (whichever political party reigned at a given time). It was a serious national problem that became a malignant cancer with a profound hold on the politics of our country.

The people who were caught in this culture thought they had real power and authority. What they didn't know was they were being misused and treated as ignorant citizens by the politicians. They were determined to prey on their ignorance. With the passage of time, the culture had taken its toll on the mind-set of some of the intelligentsia of our country.

My initial tenure in Moyamba was punctuated with trials and tensions. Moyamba was the birthplace of the late President Stevens, and any civil servant assigned to this district worked under the scrutiny of his relatives. They could be removed without questions asked.

If a civil servant was unjustly accused to the old man, that would be the end of their assignment in Moyamba. A mere telephone call to the "Pa," as he was fondly known, would be enough to get them out of Moyamba, or even out of their job.

President Stevens often used an effective strategy of playing the nationalist card. He used to joke that his great-grandparents had been born in all the provinces. There were Presidential Guest Houses in Daru, Pujehun, and Kono, to name a few. Not only that, the president spoke the three main local languages fluently.[52]

I found myself as a resident magistrate in this kind of atmosphere, quite strange to the ethics and etiquette of my professional practise. However, I was determined to break this despotic scenario once and forever. I was coming from a different cultural background where civil servants, and that includes members of the judiciary, were neutral, and therefore such neutrality must be respected.

No amount of political influence or affiliation should interfere with the execution of the duties of civil servants. The logic behind the neutrality and freedom of civil servants as well as members of the judiciary is simple. It not only nourishes and sustains democracy, its practice guarantees the sanity of any nation.

My first encounter involved Patrick Swarray, the regional secretary of the all-powerful ruling APC government, led by President Siaka Stevens. He was a powerful man in the region and well respected by the party hierarchy.

One day, a matter was brought before my court involving a party activist who fell foul of the law. A preliminary report was made by the police to the court, and in my discretion, I remanded the fellow in custody until the next hearing.

Within twenty-four hours, I received a letter from Swarray, questioning my authority to preside over a matter involving a party activist without informing him (the regional secretary) in the first instance.

When I practised in Jamaica, I never witnessed such blatant interference with the course of justice. I was determined to have this fellow apprehended and charged with contempt of court.

I quickly ordered his arrest and demanded that he be brought before me in court within forty-eight hours.

At the time, Secretary Swarray was living in the Bonthe District; he was arrested and whisked to my court in Moyamba.

Swarray was taken to the Moyamba District Prison, where he spent the weekend, and he was ordered to appear before me the next Monday morning. The news of the arrest of the most feared gentleman in the region spread like a hurricane. This was a powerful man in the ruling government.

As a consequence, the district members of Parliament (MPs), led by Harry Williams, sent a seething message to President Stevens, demanding my immediate removal as resident magistrate. He further suggested to the president that I should not only be sacked but deported to Jamaica, where I came from.

He thought I was a Jamaican by birth. I was accused of being a foreigner, with no respect for the traditions and customs of the district. Interestingly, most people in the Moyamba District perceived me as Jamaican because I platted my hair, a unique and popular practice among some Jamaicans.

The president discussed the matter with his vice president, S. I. Koroma, who explained to the president who I was and where I came from. The vice president told the president that my late father was Paramount Chief Kande Turay of Sanda, and he added that those who knew him well would attest that I carried my father's genes, meaning "Like father, like son" (a claim that was not completely accurate).

I stood my ground, in order to protect the integrity of my principles and the etiquette of my profession. While the MPs were spouting negative vibes against me, Swarray was still in prison throughout the weekend; he was scheduled to appear before me the following Monday.

On that blessed day, everyone was amazed; they were anxious to see whether this influential secretary general of the ruling party would appear. The courtroom was full to capacity. Politicians, chiefs, elders, youths, women, people from all walks of life came to see whether what they heard was real. They wanted to see this dare-devil magistrate who dared to put things right in the district for the first time during the reign of President Stevens.

When Swarray was presented to the court and placed in the dock, I read the letter to him and asked him if he had written it. He said yes, and I asked him again to tell me why I should not send him down for contempt of my court. The accused was full of remorse and apologised profusely. I then got him to promise to never again interfere with the course of justice because of his political standing.

That was not all. It was ingrained in the culture, so there was another case. This time, it was an incident punctuated by political interference. The innocent victim was an eighty-year-old man. He had been mercilessly beaten to a pulp and had his right wrist broken by the orders of the Paramount Chief and his chiefdom elders. Like the first case, the Paramount Chief and his elders were politically connected, and so they were convinced that whatever crime they committed had the blessings of the president and his ruling party.

The matter was reported to the police in Moyamba by two daughters of the poor victim. His only offence, they claimed, was that he failed to stay indoors when the local devil, known as the "Gbangbani," left the bush and entered the village. It was profane, an abominable act.

It was appalling, to say the least. In reality, the Paramount Chief and his elders were the very ones who infringed on the privacy of the old man. He was having a rest in his hammock in the veranda of his own house. They insisted that since he was not a member of this secret society, he should go indoors. He declined, and because of his refusal to leave, he was arrested, beaten up, and taken to the Paramount Chief, where he was again severely beaten, resulting in a broken wrist.

It was an open secret in most of these areas that the very custodians of the law and justice, the police, sometimes connived with the culprits against an assailant or victim. For instance, when the eighty-year-old man's daughters reported the case to the police, they were slapped in the face. The police took ages to investigate because of fear of the Paramount Chief, due to the fact that he was a cousin of President Stevens.

However, pressure came from some quarters that caused charges to be proffered against the Paramount Chief and some of his chiefdom elders.

The accused was brought before me to answer to the charges, ranging from wounding with intent to common assault.

At the preliminary hearing, all the accused persons were remanded in custody for a week. Two days later, a report was made to President Stevens. This report falsely claimed that I had ordered the entire chiefdom hierarchy locked up in prison.

President Stevens treated it as a matter of urgency. He rushed down to Moyamba in order to verify what had happened.

I had heard wind of the president's arrival in connection with the case. Again, I was determined to stay with the principles of justice and defend them at all cost. Hence, while the president was on his way, I went to pay a scheduled visit to the Shenge area within the same district.

This was done deliberately. Apparently, all government officials in the district were sitting on tenterhooks. Besides, they were beneficiaries of the disruptive political culture. Late that night, the district officer hurriedly came, on the instruction of the president, to bring me back to Moyamba.

I was determined to make a point once and for all. I declined to go back to the town until after the inspection of the disputed land in the morning. The completely distraught district officer was on his knees, pleading with me to travel back to Moyamba that night. I decided not to, so I stood my ground firmly.

The next day, after the inspection of the disputed land, we travelled back to Moyamba together. It was arranged for me to meet the president that evening. As I arrived at the residence of the president, I observed a huge crowd of chiefs, chiefdom people, elders, government officials, police personnel, and several onlookers.

I bowed down and greeted the president politely, as a matter of courtesy. You could imagine the head of state's body language towards an unknown magistrate, who'd refused to report to him immediately. He looked at me contemptuously, but I simply smiled.

He threw a question at me: "I understand you are presiding over a matter that has to do with customary and traditional values. And that you have the guts to remand in custody the natural ruler, the head, I mean, the Chief Custodian of the very customs and traditions of the people of this chiefdom? You have the audacity to lock up the Paramount Chief of this chiefdom?"

Then he took a hard look at me once more and asked me a single question in a sharp, angry voice: "Why?"

My reply was simple but justified and informative. I said, in a respectful tone, "Your Excellency, the Sierra Leone Constitution quite clearly and unequivocally made separation of powers fundamental. The Executive, the Judiciary, and the Legislative—each has a level to operate. These three arms are quite independent of each other. Therefore, Your Excellency, with great respect, if I had done anything wrong in terms of the law, the correct body to be contacted would be the Head of the Judiciary, i.e., the Chief Justice, who, in turn, through the Master and Registrar, would ask me to explain."[53]

I reiterated in my conclusion quite unequivocally, "Your Excellency, sir, the Chief Justice is indeed the correct medium to contact me. However, with great respect, sir, being my head of state, I would humbly answer your question."

After that, I said, "Your Excellency, the matter before me involved charges of wounding with intent, wounding, occasioning actual bodily

66

harm, and common assault of an eighty-year-old man. It was not a matter involving the violation of customs and traditions of the said chiefdom." Then I referred to the charge sheet presented to the court by the police, in order to make my point and justify my action.

It was a fierce encounter to say the least. Above all, it took President Stevens and his kinsmen by surprise. When I stopped, I could see anger radiating from the face of the president. His demeanour had changed completely. He then spoke to the police officer in charge at the time. The police were on the side of the law, so they were discreet in their explanation and presentation to His Excellency. The police officer confirmed without a shadow of doubt the charges they proffered after their investigation of the matter.

It was at this juncture that hell broke loose. The president turned to me and said, "Young magistrate, please send them all to prison for life."

Most significantly, President Stevens entreated me to continue to do the good work I was assigned to do in the Moyamba District.

No matter how uncomfortable it was, the whole scenario went down as a landmark in the discharge of my duties in Moyamba. First, I didn't succumb to the pressure of injustice. Second, I defended the integrity of the judiciary of Sierra Leone and the laws of the land. Third, my behaviour sent a clear message that officials of the Crown should not compromise the sanctimonious edicts of their jobs due to political pressure from above.

My actions also went a long way to justify the point that if we held tight to the values and virtues of national unity and discipline in all that we do, Sierra Leone would remain a better place for all of us to enjoy the fruits of our talents and contributions. Since that day, I became an unofficial advisor to the president, up to the time of his death. This encounter set the tone for our relationship in other areas of my endeavours.

Any time he visited Moyamba, he would invite me to his residence for a chat. He would ask for my opinion on certain state matters.

Through that period, not once did I say what he wanted to hear. I sincerely expressed my opinion and suggested solutions. I had a very close relationship with him, and that paid off in my later political development.

Another case of contempt of court became known as "Pa Trye and the Typewriter."[54] The culprit was an old man named Pa Trye. He was an infamous character, a social mischief, notorious for spying and reporting all government officials in Moyamba to the his close friend, the president. His notoriety became a cliché, by which was called "Pa Trye and the Typewriter." Any civil servant who fell foul with the community elders of Moyamba would be transferred immediately based on the typewritten report of the infamous Pa Trye.

One day, I found a letter mistakenly addressed to me. I noted it was a typewritten letter addressed to President Stevens and signed by Pa Trye. In that letter, Pa Trye said all sorts of negative things about me personally and against my official status as the magistrate of Moyamba District. He recommended my immediate removal from Moyamba.

After reading the letter, I instructed my court clerk to issue a subpoena for Pa Trye to appear in court the following day. The news went round the township like wild fires during the dry season in tropical Africa. By the time I arrived in the court, the whole area was packed full to capacity. Pa Trye was docked. I showed him a copy of the letter and asked if it was his signature, which he confirmed. I asked him to read the letter aloud for the whole court to hear. He did so with inaudible sounds when he read the most damaging parts of the letter. I then insisted that he speak loudly and clearly.[55]

He was embarrassed. At the end of it all, I put the question to him: "Give me a tangible reason why the court should not send you down for contempt." The old man was shaking terribly, like a weathered leaf. He begged the court for mercy.

I was very professional in my questioning, in order to create the desired effect and serve as a corrective measure. I wanted all the culprits who were used to this divisive culture to desist from it. My first question was well measured and precise: "Pa Trye the Typewriter, are you one of the old people in town who always communicates with the president to smear the character of young civil servants posted to work in Moyamba?"[56]

When this was followed by many salient and poignant questions, he confessed to all he'd done in past—all the damage he'd done to the good names and characters of his victims, the civil servants. In the end, I came to the conclusion that he showed genuine signs of remorse. Pa Trye the Typewriter vouched never to do anything like that again in his lifetime.

The fact is that Pa Trye the Typewriter was not the only character assassin in the Moyamba District. And Moyamba District was not the place where such social vices had roots. It was a common phenomenon around the country. It was one of the effects of the neo-patrimonial culture. Poverty could be one of the many explanations.

People had to devise any means in order to gain access to the corridors of power and secure their livelihoods.

I made my point and sent a very strong message to all and sundry. Pa Trye the Typewriter, the social mischief, had got the message more than anyone else. Hence, I sympathised with his situation once he'd shown remorse and undertaken a vow never to repeat the same, and to desist from it and make amends. Since then the habit died out in Moyamba. Civil servants are free to go about their genuine jobs without fear or favour.

CHAPTER 7

POLITICS ON THE HORIZON

———————⟶◦⟵———————

"In human endeavours, especially in politics, crossing
the Rubicon means no turning back no matter how the
going gets tough."

Eddie Turay, Recounting Past Challenges

I was now at the crucibles; there was no turning back. Since politics
had beckoned visibly, it was time to hit the nail on the head. The
most important figure whose favour I had to win at all cost was the
president. In retrospect, there were no obstacles in my way, as far as I
could envision. I became a close confidant of President Siaka Stevens.
Apparently, he'd been captivated by my professionalism and stern
principles. And those facts would put me in good stead, without a
shadow of doubt. The foundation had been laid; it was just a matter
of when to start the construction of the edifice. In other words, I had
to back my intentions with a practical stance, not words and mere
dreams.

Luckily, the Moyamba scenario was the beginning of the captivation,
warmth, and trust he later manifested in me. For a leader of his calibre,
I must confess that I was surprised that he was that at ease with me.

He would discuss a variety of topics without reservation, the law, politics, women, the effects of youth unemployment, and a host of other related issues.

In the course of some of these discussions, we also discussed national representatives in the various constituencies in the country. His regime had assumed power at the time Sierra Leone was still a young nation politically. He was a clever operator, a shrewd politician to say the least.

His questions were poignant. For example, he asked, "Who is the member of Parliament where you live?" I gave a straight answer: "His Excellency, the incumbent is Thaimu Bangura."

He said, "Thaimu who?" He pondered a bit, twisted his nose left to right, and then said, "Oh, the tall guy who spoke a lot at Cabinet meetings with little or no substance. He sometimes irritated me. I realised that the question had a hidden undertone; he was trying to go under my skin, psyche me, and ascertain whether I had any political ambitions.

Then all of a sudden, he asked if I had ever thought of becoming a politician. I told him the thought never came to my mind, for two reasons:

"If I opted now for politics," I said, "I would have to resign from the Civil Service less than two years of my three year contract with the government, and in that case I would have to refund to the government of Sierra Leone the cost of my repatriation from the UK, totalling £4000 Sterling, and I have no money of my own to venture into politics, let alone talk of contesting an election."

He smiled, reflected a bit, and then said quite clearly, "I will certainly give you financial and moral support, just as I did for Abass Bundu and others."

He also assured me that he would refund the £4000. In those days, that amount was the equivalent of Le 8000 in Sierra Leone's local currency.

That was not the end of His Excellency's generosity; he even promised to finance my campaign.

"If it is the refund that is holding you back," he said, "then rest assured that I will take care of it, and that will grant you the freedom to contest."[57]

On reflection, I realised from the conversations with the president and the pointed questions he asked about the incumbent that the Honourable Thaimu Bangura was not in his good books. I seized the opportunity and decided to run for the seat, against the incumbent, Thaimu Bangura.

Having given him my consent, henceforth I became a very close friend of the statesman. I was given priority access to the president at the State House any time I called to see him. The cordiality and camaraderie between us raised a few eyebrows. Almost all the senior civil servants in the office of the president knew me and called me "the president's outside son" (or, if you like, his "son out of wedlock").

The waiting game of diplomacy was over. I decided to make my intentions public. After all, the president and leader of the ruling party had given me his blessings; why wait any more? I declared my intentions to contest in my village, Gbanti, amidst pomp and pageantry. My people mere tremendously happy about the public declaration; it went down well.

The news went down well for me. But mind you, the saying goes, look before you leap. I didn't resign my job immediately. I was still the resident magistrate of Moyamba. My opponents, including the incumbent, of course, went on the offensive immediately.

Suddenly I received a hint from Alhaji Mamodu Munu in the Office of the Establishment Secretary that I would not be eligible to contest because my contract of repatriation from the UK to Sierra Leone was still active, and as a result, I would not be released until I repaid the cost of my repatriation.

Quite understandably, there was a culture of exclusion among the clique that surrounded the president. It was similar to tribal politics, which is often advanced and nurtured not to promote the national interests. Rather, it was a catalyst for the promotion of self-interest. I was not going to have any of it. I was a member of the All People's Congress (APC), and so to allow someone to bully me would sound foolish and cowardly on my part.

Not meaning to be misconstrued in any sense of the word, I do not say this to mean that the APC of that period was an exclusive and elitist political club. Reading the history of political parties, their practices and cultures, elitism was not peculiar to any particular political party. But comparatively speaking, the APC was quite the opposite.

Ours is a Socialist party with strong social democratic leanings and particularities. We are very much inclusive. Therefore, we practice liberalism and seek the national interests by creating an enabling and inclusive environment within and without our party. The fact that most of the current senior members of the other parties have served as senior cabinet ministers under the leadership of Stevens and Saidu Momoh justifies my assertion.

Inclusive politics and seeking the national interests characterise our party. They are the centre piece of the rationales which inform the philosophy and ideology of our party and leadership. Our founder and leader, President Stevens, stood firmly by these values. He went all out to make sure during his lifetime that politics touched every Sierra Leonean. Indeed, that is the real difference in regional origins, ethnicity and social status notwithstanding.

I sought the candid opinions of the liberal-minded members of the inner circle of the party. They advised me to inform the president without delay. I called the Pa and informed him accordingly, and within an hour, he invited me to see him at the State House. Not many politicians, let alone a head of state, would do such a thing. But that was the nature and character of the man. He was down to earth in his approach, especially when it had to do with party politics.

What marked Stevens from previous leaders is that he was a pragmatist. Thus, the moment I got to the State House, he wasted no time but counted the Le 8000 and passed it on to me to pay for my release from the Civil Service. It was to further buttress his promise in support of my political ambitions.

It came as a bombshell, an utter shock to most people, including some in the party hierarchy. For instance, when Alhaji Munu heard about the payment, he was shocked. So many permutations must have overwhelmed his thoughts. Who could have paid the money? Had I nurtured political ambitions while studying abroad? Did I have an external financier? Was I financed by the president? If so, why did he? Why was he trying to finance my political ambition? Would that not count as a conflict of interest in the party? If he sponsored the refunds, that would mean he wanted to replace the incumbent; why would he want to do that?

I resigned from the service and entered active politics. The political battle in the Sanda region was born. The warriors were all members of the same political party, the APC, as we were under a single political party system.

The advantage in favour of the party, despite all the risky politics at the time, was that it was very popular. And the popularity cut across regional and ethnic politics. On my own part, the fact is that come what may, I had crossed the Rubicon, and there was no turning back. The battle lines were drawn.

CHAPTER 8

APC VERSUS APC: PHASE ONE

———◁◉▷———

"Man must evolve for all human conflict a method which rejects revenge, aggression, and retaliation. The foundation of such a method is love."

Dr Martin Luther King Jr.

The General Elections of 1982[58] were unique for three key reasons. First, it was condemned as the most violent elections in the political history of Sierra Leone. Second, it was fought under the umbrella of a one-party system of government. The APC was the only political party at the time, by legislation.

In theory, we were all supposed to be members of the same political family, the same political fraternity, the APC Party. Third, it was fought literally on the basis of brother against brother due to the fact that Sierra Leone was virtually a single-party democracy.

I would also add that its significance showed that the single-party system of government was found grossly wanton. Sierra Leoneans had failed to evolve for our national conflicts a credible method that rejects revenge, aggression, and retaliation. Personally, what I learned from this dysfunctional phenomenon was that violence is not the sine qua non of our problems.

The elections were organised into two phases, primaries and secondary, during which the final votes were cast by the electorates. As soon as the date was fixed for the elections, the whole country erupted into a political frenzy—primaries were held in various constituencies. They were marred by violence, as it was the order of the day. Like a hurricane, it engulfed everyone, from the top to the bottom among the party functionaries.

At the primaries, the fates of the aspiring candidates were in the hands of the party executive members.[59] They were mandated to elect the candidates of their choice. I must warn that the process was not as straightforward as it sounds. It involved combinations of politicking as well as lethal violence, especially in strategic constituencies. More often than not, the post-primaries, that is the times when the elections proper were conducted, were even trickier and more problematic. Both the party functionaries and voters had to fight vehemently for their respective candidates.

There were three of us that billed to contest the elections in the Bombali Central Constituency: Thaimu Bangura (the incumbent), Dr Abdulai Timbo, and myself. Of the two, Dr Timbo was a soft torch. He was match for both of us. My main opponent was the incumbent. But here is the catch: since Thaimu Bangura recognised the strength of my candidacy, the real political battle was between him and Dr Timbo.

It was a complex and very complicated political climate the three of us had to face. Amazingly, the realities and wider ramifications didn't go by any textbook lessons. The three of us were at each other's throats. However, the other two candidates thought they could do business with me.

It was apparent that each thought I could be a safe pair of hands. Hence, I took advantage of the situation and played an immense game of diplomacy. I maintained a good political relationship with both candidates, though in reality it was a front. They didn't know that I was a shrewd politician who could pass easily for the venom of a poisonous rattlesnake.

I must warn readers, however, that though I was a political rattlesnake as required by a given situation and political climate, political violence is not my cup of tea. It is not my nature; I don't celebrate violence as a means of acquiring political power. In fact, it was for that reason that I chose to go into politics: eliminate violence and clean up politics. My aim was to gain as many allies as I can, clean up the politics of our country, and create an enabling environment for my compatriots.

Making reference to Mahatma Gandhi as one of the sources of my inspirations to do politics without violence, the great man once said:

"I object to violence because when it appears to do well, the good is only temporary, the evil it does is permanent."

However, that doesn't mean that I am not capable of reacting to situations. Besides, by virtue of the political climate and nature, all of us had supports that were very unpredictable. We had virtually no control over them. Bangura was conscious of this fact. He knew that he could not in any way use violence against me, because my supporters would retaliate vehemently to the extent that it would be indiscriminate.

But that wouldn't stop him. He'd read the texts in and out and was capable of posing surprises. On this particular occasion, knowing too well the political climate was tense, and that one of his opponents (myself) had predatory political instincts, and that there was a lot at stake, the incumbent had other ideas. He engaged in manipulating voters and played the tribal or ethnic card seriously.

It was a miscalculation, especially because the electorate had had enough of it. They were looking out for substance, one that could be translated into concrete socio-economic benefits for them and their children. They were ready to listen to substantiated proposals to bring about economic development for their constituency and the Bombali District.

Hence, this time playing on tribal sentiments was less effective, to say the least. This was how he planned to unleash the tribal strategy as a weapon to win votes. Dr Abdul Timbo is an ethnic Fullah, while Thaimu and I are Temnes. The implications: the majority of the electorate are ethnic Temnes. Also in terms of voters' registration, only a small fraction of Fullah and Susus were registered voters in the constituency.[60]

I was determined to hold the balance of power and eliminate both candidates if I had the upper hand. Thus, I decided to deviate from tribal sentiments, open up, and maximise the potential of the educated class. In my campaign camp, I recruited teachers, secondary school pupils, and civil servants. I calculated very well, knowing that these were respectable groups, and that would send a clear message that my political platform was to reform and clean the system, not vandalise and corrupt people's minds.

I did my level best to be a reforming candidate on this basis, but once political violence was ingrained in the constituency, it was difficult to bring about finesse. It was business as usual. The day when the primaries were to be held to elect the candidates for the Bombali Central Constituency, unprecedented violence erupted between our supporters. Each camp tried to block the opponent's candidate from taking part in the primary.

Again, I tried very hard to keep my camp out of the violence and its machinations. Unfortunately, it became clear that Thaimu's camp was determined to spread the violence. Before we realised it, they had effectively blocked Dr Timbo's camp from participating in the primaries. He used the ethnic advantage: Temnes against the Fullah and Susus minorities.

They say coming events cast their shadows. I was alert and used every precaution at my disposal. I sensed the danger that Thaimu would turn to my camp and do likewise. How correct we were; indeed, we learnt later on that the incumbent had put a lethal plan in place to unleash mayhem on my camp.

I have to reiterate that violence is neither my nature nor my political strategy. As a trained lawyer, discipline, the basis of safeguarding the constitution, and its application for the betterment of all and sundry are part and parcel of my professional training.

I also have to enlighten those who are aware of the political culture in Sierra Leone at the time under discussion that most candidates did not per se preside over political violence. In those days, party supporters, especially the diehards, were powerful. They had the elections in their hands, especially when it comes to political strategies and electioneering. One could look at in an unconventional way of being akin to military tactics.

Thus, it was unlike the modern, conventional military tactics sense, which are well planned by the commanders and generals, and then the troops are left with the assignments to execute them. In the scenario I am talking about, a docile, law-abiding political strategist (candidate)-cum-military general or commander, the executors (troops, supporters) on the field may choose to do otherwise.

There is equally an explanation for the manners or psyches of the troops, foot soldiers of the candidates, in the process of execution, that is, being on the offensive against the opponents' counter-attacks. The political milieu at the time was fluid, violent, and politically non-conformist by nature. It was very much deregulated, in that every Tom, Dick, and Harry did what they liked as long as they delivered the goods in the end: election victory.

Therefore, these foot soldiers were unfortunate victims of history. How could they have chosen to dig their own graves? It is pathetic! Innocent lives were lost, properties were destroyed, and hatred became deep-seated as the divisive consequences, the wider ramification of the disorderly, dysfunctional politics that was at play at the time.

The situation in Moyamba was similar. I had the guts to take the chances I took and challenged the system, simply because I am qualified and well equipped to stand on my own feet. For the innocent youths, they were without skills and qualifications. Their only means of survival were to become thugs, hired mercenaries, sent to run the dirty errands: rig elections. Sadly, thousands died in the process. In effect, they were used as cogs in the political machinery. I have to say that those were the realities of that cruel political history.

Coming back to the reaction of my camp against my key opponent's moves, a pre-emptive and fearless attack was organised even before I knew it. The essence was not to kill but to neutralise his planned attacks. With dismay, I must say, it evaporated into despicable violence: properties were destroyed, villages were burnt down, and a mass exodus of people fled from Rosanda. Both camps suffered casualties.

Of course, the logic is simple: in every attack, pre-emptive or otherwise, both camps must suffer casualties and collateral damage. The battle was fierce, and my camp had the upper hand in terms of wading off Thaimu Bangura and his foot soldiers and mercenaries. They retreated, and it became the talk of the entire country. Our victory was on the lips of everyone in every household. They celebrated the impregnability of our constituency and hailed it in our local parlance: *"Rosanda Pikin Nor for go day,"* a slogan meaning, "Rosanda is a no-go area for kids."[61]

What was the next strategy by Thaimu Bangura? I must confess that he was a recalcitrant politician. He never gave up easily, which made him a true product of the system. His resolve was unshakable, and whatever he initiated, he pursued to the core. The paradox is one wonders why he didn't utilise such resources for the progress and socio-economic development of his constituency and country. Perhaps this major flaw was behind the president's dislike of him.

Having failed in his attempt to dislodge my camp and cheat his way at the polls, he endorsed the intervention of the security forces. He wanted to weaken the morale of members of my camp. They tried to make arrests, but they were overwhelmed and beaten off from the scene.

The APC was the only ruling party at the time. All other political parties, including the main opposition, the Sierra Leone People's Party (SLPP), had all been relegated to the political wilderness. Some of her key members were now made cabinet ministers in Stevens's government. Veteran politicians like Dr Sama Banya (alias Puawei) and a host of others took up posts in the only political party in the country.

The derivative Puawei![62] Dr Sama Banya's nickname was actually given to him by President Stevens. According to the story, it was during the hosting of an OAU conference in Sierra Leone. President Stevens had appointed Dr Banya minister of Finance and Economic Affairs.

During his tenure at these two key ministries, combined into one cabinet post, the weight of the job overwhelmed him. It took a toll on his physical make-up; he looked older in appearance than his age. Visibly, his nice, golden bushy hair turned from black to silver.

In the veteran politician's ethnic Mende language, "Puawei" means "silver [or gray] hair." That was how he acquired the name, and he proudly uses it to this day as his penname. He uses it for his articles in the *Sierra Leone Awareness Times* and other tabloids.

It has been argued that the APC was its own nemesis, since there were no other official parties to oppose it, except its intermittent internal political feuds. There were internal camps created more along petty jealousies than ideological beliefs. However, the fact of the matter is that these things happen in politics, differences in geography and economic status notwithstanding. Tony Blair's New Labour Party had fragmentary camps, which eventually boiled over, compounded by ideological divides.

Similar trends prevailed in Stevens's APC. He had absolute control over his government, but there were petty cracks in party management and in the hierarchy, due to the malignant diatribe culture, which wasn't going away. For instance, as in my case, the president and his vice presidents had different opinions as well as preferential candidates.

Some MPs and cabinet ministers had divided loyalties as a result of this problem. I enjoyed the support and backing of the president, while Thaimu Bangura was supported by the vice president, Sorie Ibrahim (S. I.) Koroma. His critics infamously referred to him as "Agba Satani," a satanic connotation, meaning politically satanic and manipulative (Wundah, 2004).

It was a precarious situation for the president and his vice president. They not only gave us moral support, they backed it with financial sponsorship. The president threw his financial muscle behind me and my camp. His vice president did likewise for the incumbent. It was an open secret, on everyone's lips in every household.

I also believed that the security forces knew about this salient point, so they never took sides. Now and again, all they could do was play diplomat and hold neutral roles in the event of renewed clashes and eruption of violence between me and Thaimu Bangura.

Our problems lingered, and our two godfathers continued to nurture our division. Once in a while, we would bother them with complaints. Unfortunately, no redress was forthcoming. The political impasse in Bombali Central Constituency continued unabated.

After one of my numerous complaints against the incumbent, the president told me this: "It is only the weak cowards that spend time explaining the nature of their defeat. First and foremost, never allow defeat to consume you. Fight on, until victory is yours. You must always fight on with one aim—the defeat of the opponent." Then he gave me a gentle pat on my shoulder before I left his premises.

The president's admonitions reminded me of what my late father always said: "Don't bow to cowardice; be still and fight for your right and for others. Justice favours the brave and just."

At the time, the whole country knew that S. I. Koroma was very faithful and would do whatever the president told him. Hence, he could only advise Thaimu Bangura to be very careful and to reflect on why I had no fear to attack him wherever and whenever we met. Thaimu needed to know the answer, and S. I. Koroma advised him to be careful.

At the conclusion of the primaries, all three of us were awarded the ticket to fight it out in Bombali Central Constituency.

As the 1982 elections were approaching and voting days steadily came nearer, violence erupted across the constituency; my first pre-emptive action was to advise the vice president to stay neutral in the political fight between Thaimu and me. S. I. Koroma, like the president, was a very sensible politician. He listened to my advice

At the close of the polls, Thaimu knew he had lost the elections, and his supporters (including polling agents and other officials) decided to rig the elections. They seized all the ballot boxes in his strongholds and stuffed them with ballot papers. The Electoral Commissioners were appalled. Having stuffed them to their heart's desires; they took them to Thaimu Bangura's campaign headquarters in his village.

When I heard the news, I rushed to Thaimu's village with a huge crowd of supporters, but before we got to his village, he was tipped by an insider in our camp and fled to Makeni. We chased him there, and the two camps went into fierce battle. The police simply watched as spectators; they advised both camps to travel to Freetown and submit reports to the authorities.

Later, some of the boxes were found broken, sufficient enough to cancel the polls. Unfortunately, they were still dispatched to Freetown and later transferred to Siaka Stevens Stadium for counting.

I made a report to the president, who then sought a confirmation from the Electoral Commission about the allegation of broken seals in Bombali Central ballot boxes. After this was confirmed, the commission ordered the immediate cancellation of the vote. A bye election was ordered at a later date.

These events should not be misconstrued as national failures on the part of President Stevens. As Sierra Leoneans, we have our views, and they are different and extremely contentious. I would like to judge Stevens's term in context. To most people in both the party and the country, Stevens was an enigma. He was mystifying, baffling, perplexing, impenetrable, equivocal, paradoxical, obscure, oblique, and secretive. In reality, President Stevens was all of these synonymous adjectival descriptions.

For instance, in his heyday, the president was at times paradoxical in the manner in which he treated certain matters and serious policies. Those who know the politics of Bombali District and who know Thaimu Bangura and I, who fought it out for the right to be awarded the party symbol, would be left with nothing other than a serious concern over the manner in which he initially handled it.

It was marred by contradictions; at first, it appeared he supported me wholeheartedly, only to back down and support his vice president's choice, my opponent. On the other hand, one would argue that it was the politics of the absolute disguise.

And should that be the case, there were too many such disguises which created concerns about his political judgment. Failings! Under his leadership, the country, like most countries in the Third World, may have been marred in the lingering troubles of the Cold War, but one can still point to some concrete development schemes which were developed by the president.

The Sierra Leone National Stadium and the national water supply project in the North (though hampered by economic constraints and compounded by mismanagement) are two of the many projects. Above, considering the Socialist ideology of the APC, Siaka Stevens and his team made it an inclusive party. Opportunities in the party were not limited to the demands of political nepotism.

CHAPTER 9

THE PRIMARIES OF THE BYE ELECTIONS

—◦—

"I believe that unarmed truth and unconditional love will have the final word in reality. That is why right, temporarily defeated, is stronger than evil triumphant."

Dr Martin Luther King Jr.

The bye-election primaries were again held in Makeni, with the three of us as the contestants. My supporters and I were amazed at the conclusion, when Thaimu Bangura emerged as the candidate. It came about as a result of the intervention of the vice president, S. I. Koroma. He used a hundred and one strategies to make sure that I was deselected.

It was high politics, and inherent logic couldn't be ignored. Thaimu Bangura and I are Temnes, while Dr Timbo is Fullah. The implication is that two Temne candidates were at war, instead of forming a united front to fight Dr Timbo.

The president gave us a stock warning and asked us to step in line.

"If you continue with this madness," he warned us, "you will split the votes of your traditional strongholds, the Temnes." As we both nodded our heads, he continued, "Not only that, both of you will end up offering Dr Timba victory on a silver platter, because he will have his Fullah and Susus ethnic groups to vote for him and combine those votes with the ones he would get from your split camps."[63]

That was not all; there were more political twists and turns, and some serious critical horse trading in the entire saga. Both S. I. Koroma and the president had to make some personal sacrifices. In another constituency marred by similar tensions, the vice president had his own candidate, and President Stevens's choice was Dr Abass Bundu.

The president told the vice president to withdraw his candidate in favour of Dr Abass Bundu, for whom the president had considerable admiration. In return, Koroma requested that the president withdraw my candidacy in favour of Thaimu Bangura. In effect, I was a victim of a political barter system. Of course, I was deeply disappointed, but that is politics for you.

It was my turn to sit on the sidelines as an observer of the emerging saga. This was utterly unfamiliar territory for me, since my father had admonished me to never, ever give up a fight, no matter the magnitude and implications. This one was utterly different, a different kettle of fish for any sane person's consumption.

Thaimu Bangura and Dr Timbo were now left in the race as the two candidates for the bye election. Their campaigns were marred by tribal feuds and unprecedented violence. The violence was dubbed the Temne-Fullah war. The Temnes are traditionally farmers, while the Fullahs are cattle herders. Hence, it was effectively a battle between farmers and cattle herders. Since the Temnes are in the majority, they had the upper hand over the Fullah minority.

The conflict reached fever pitch to the extent that they displaced most of the Fullahs. It is not that the Fullahs didn't have political capital; they did, for most of them had amassed wealth out of their cattle trade.

And as they say, wealth begets political power; no wonder they were eager to have their tribesman, Dr Timbo, win the elections.

The two candidates played the tribal card, inciting one tribe after the other for political gains. Thamu's theory was simple: If the Temnes allowed the political baton to pass over to the Fullahs, the constituency would be covered by herds of cows, and farming would be a thing of the past. The cows of the Fullahs would feed on the growing rice fields.

Due to the uneven tribal composition, the campaign was one sided. The supporters of Dr Timbo were restricted to their minority areas, as the Temnes made roadblocks all over the constituency. On voting day, the Fullahs were not allowed to vote in many polling stations; inevitably, the winner was the incumbent, Thaimu Bangura. That was the end of the chapter. Bangura won an election marred by violence and political intrigue.

I had given up a race marred by violence, costing many lives and the destruction of property. However, I didn't give up; in fact, I had other ideas. After the bye election, I went to see the old Pa (President Stevens) in order to express my disappointment. He was apologetic and asked me what I wanted him to do for me.

The president presented me many options to choose from. They included the position of chief justice of Sierra Leone or a diplomatic post in West Germany. It was an exciting time, and the choices were very tempting. But I reflected on the advice of my late father. So I thanked him for both offers and asked for time in order to consult my family and supporters.

The offer of becoming chief justice of Sierra Leone came across as extremely contentious. Not that I didn't have the qualifications or necessary skills, but I thought there were political as well as professional implications, had I chosen it. The Sierra Leone judiciary at the time was dominated by the Creoles, our western brothers,. And for a young Temne man from Sanda to assume that position at the time, purely because of my political affiliation to the president, would have amounted to legal suicide.[64]

Hence, I declined the first offer. The second offer, ambassador to West Germany, was also not ideal for one reason: politics had now taken my soul and spirit, and I opted to stay at home to prepare for the next elections in 1986.

Also, I recalled one of the sayings of my late father: "Never betray the trust of those who risk their lives and stand by you at your crucial time."

And there was another saying that always brought sweet laughter out of me, no matter how distraught I was: "The sun shines on those who stand before it shines on those who kneel."[65] This saying was very relevant vis-à-vis the manner I looked at the president's proposal to appoint me chief justice of Sierra Leone.

On the basis of the reflections of the great man, my deceased father, I kept faith with my constituents, as they had done with me. One thing I realised throughout the battle between me and my political opponents in the Bombali Central Constituency is that I envisioned a natural bond, one that glued everyone together.

On many, many occasions, the members of the constituency told me that they stood by me through thick and thin as a concrete symbol of the love they had for my father and their unshakable devotion to him, even in death.

One of my father's elders once told me this in confidence: "Your late father was our unfailing, trusted friend, hero, mouthpiece. Your father was the most reliable defender of our faith. In that consummate role, not once did he betray us, so we shall never, ever betray you."[66]

The next four years, I spent a lot of time visiting the constituency. These visits often saw intermittent clashes between my supporters and those of the incumbent, Thaimu Bangura. Sanda was declared a no go political zone, and the government of Siaka Stevens pretended as if nothing happened. The police knew the political status of the two Sanda brothers, and so they also turned a blind eye. The violence became so deadly that the government had to do something about it.

Both the president and his vice president were aware of the fact that I was popular in our constituency. It became glaring that they both may have succeed in controlling the populace through the manipulations of machine politics, but what they couldn't dismiss, let alone sweep under the rug, was the impact of my popularity on the psyches of my people. They reckoned that both Thaimu Bangura and I were popular, and therefore our supporters wanted us to be parliamentarians at all cost.

It was through divine revelation that I thought of an idea which could resolve the impasse and end the bloodshed in our constituency. During one of my personal meetings with President Stevens, after I was relegated to the political wilderness, I raised the idea of delimitating the constituencies in the whole country. I compared constituencies in the South and East of the country; some districts in our area, the Northern Province, have only one or two constituencies as opposed to many constituencies in other districts.

By the time I left the presence of His Excellency, my suggestion had made an impression on him. Fortunately for myself and others in the constituencies in the Northern Province, it formed the basis of the 1986 electoral reforms.

I have to say this as a tribute to the late President Stevens: he was very much receptive to good ideas and suggestions. And he would waste no time in seeing to it that actions were taken to put them into effect. Thus, before the 1986 elections, a change was made to the constituencies, and our Bombali Central Constituency became Bombali Central 1 and Bombali Central 2.[67]

After the delimitation process, I secured a safe seat in Central 1, and Thaimu Bangura took the smaller constituency, Bombali Central 2.

In politics, people may have different views. They may either converge or diverge on views. It is one of the many benefits of a pluralistic democracy. Therefore, in my view, I would argue that, unlike the previous elections, the 1986 elections were conducted in a peaceful and cordial political climate.

There were no hassles, no conflicts, and of course no opposing contestants to worry about. It was smooth sailing. I won easily in the newly reconfigured Central 1 Constituency, and Thaimu defeated Dr Timbo in Central 2. The victory heralded the beginning of my leadership role in the APC Party.

In politics, personal feuds rarely die out; instead, they often persist till eternity. However, even though both Thaimu Bangura and I had our separate parliamentary constituencies and were elected with ease, our personal feud continued. I must say that I was the initiator of the feud, being a political realist, not an ideologue. Throughout our campaigns, which were marred by violence, I upheld one reality: responding to the call of my people. I was simply responding to their aspirations.

I know that my style is not violent. It is the case because by virtue of the ethics of my profession, I am and must be a peace lover. I am one who would lay down his life in order to secure peace and preserve human dignity through the application of the principles of justice. I have never proclaimed threat and duress as a means to an end. It is as unjustified as it is illogical. It doesn't work; it is untenable.

Echoing a popular quotation of one of the Taqi brothers during this tumultuous political period, I would say that this is my creed too: "I have fought too long in politics. My weapons have been words and the powers of convictions. Their targets have been the minds, hearts, and souls of the populace."[68]

Having said that, there is an African proverb which states, "If you cut off your head and offer it to your arch enemy in order for him to make peace with you, it is more often than not counterproductive." The irony about the feud between myself and Thaimu Bangura is that we were both members of the same party. And for this unsavoury situation to continue, even after the retirement and death of our political mentor and leader, President Stevens, was sheer madness.

Even after the ascension of President Stevens's successor, Major General Joseph Saidu Momoh, the relationship between Thaimu Bangura and me was tenuous. We were still suspicious of each other.

This was unhealthy for the party, being senior members and MPs of the party.

Most commentators have characterised President J. S. Momoh's reign as an unsuccessful one. Like all things in politics, it is contentious and very much open to debate. What we need to bear in mind is that every era in politics, as well as history, has its inherent flaws and advantages. The president came to power on the back of extremely difficult political times.

The Cold War ended after the fall of the Berlin wall. Most of the world had lingered in economic contractions. As for the Third World or developing countries, especially in Africa, we had suffered socio-economically under the heavy weight of foreign debt and lingering poverty and deprivation. These phenomena were not noticeable in the face of the more pressing and important world affairs. They included the political debates often occupied by the Cold War and nuclear disarmament.

Hence, political abuses in the North and South Divide, in terms socio-economic inequality and lack of enabling environments, were overshadowed by the global political podium, what political analysts of that age dubbed the "more pressing issues."[69] In effect, debates around nuclear weapons and the ideological war between the USSR and the West (the United States and her key ally, Great Britain) were of more concern than writing off Third World debts and lifting her out of poverty.

Prior to the advent of J. S. Momoh, pulsating cries to break the decades of political mole, that is, abolishing the country's one-party system and replacing it with democratic pluralism, was on the minds of everyone in Africa where there were repressive regimes. By the time he became president, a sense of awareness had been created among the people of Sierra Leone.

Too many sensitive and critical questions were being asked. Sensitive sessions were being conducted in communities. These were critical times, and the political climate had begun changing. During the days of President Stevens, Momoh's predecessor and mentor, people with critical minds were perceived as dissidents.

In sharp contrast, it was now the advent of a new era, an era of awareness. Open defiance was gathering pace. Sierra Leoneans started to ask questions around the themes of open democracy. The populace demanded accountability, as well as free and fair elections. They wanted an immediate end to human rights abuses due to the misuse of political power and authority by the crème de la crème. Not only that, Sierra Leoneans were deeply concerned about the deadly virus of corruption, the lingering youth unemployment, debilitating poverty and deprivation, and the age-old burden of foreign debt.

It could also be argued that Momoh's presidency was met with ill faith. There was bad luck on his part in the sense that it was during his term that the RUF rebels staged a grotesque civil conflict.

On the other hand, it could be argued that, in hindsight, even if President Stevens had not retired, the dramatic and swift changes that came in the wake of the end of the Cold War would have impacted him. Indeed, President Stevens was a shrewd, cunning, rattlesnake-like politician and leader, but the winds of change wouldn't have spared him. J. S. Momoh was an exception.

Many things happened before Peter Tucker and group of experts wrote the 1991 Constitution.[70] That constitution stipulated some crucial demands which were to be addressed immediately. One of the casualties of those uncompromising demands was the one-party system of government (J. L. Hirsch, 2001; O. A. Otunni, et al., 1998; A. T. Kabbah, 2010; Wundah, 2004).

For our party, the APC, the emerging change had wider ramifications. The one-party system of government meant that members of other political parties had no choice but to cross over. After the 1991 constitution, they now opted out of the former political marriage of convenience under the one-party political dispensation.

As a result of this new political dimension in the country, a proliferation of new political parties surfaced. In addition to the original established parties, the SLPP and the APC, other parties were born, including the Peoples' Democratic Party (PDP), led by Thaimu Bangura, the National Unity Party (NUP), and Peoples' National Party (PNP). The political atmosphere was rickety and tense. Almost half of the membership of the APC Party abandoned ship to form their own political parties.

In the midst of this political chaos, the awareness of the new political dispensation was manifest all over the country. For the first time in close to twenty-four years, multi-party elections were set to be conducted. Unfortunately, they were aborted by the military coup of 29 April 1992 (A. T. Kabbah, 2010; M. Wundah, 2004, 20111, 2012; J. L. Hirsch, 2010).

There were obvious personal implications for me and my political ambitions. At last, there was light at the end of the tunnel. Significantly, in December 1991, I was elected the national secretary general of the All Peoples' Congress Party. Apparently, the populace had virtually divorced the relationships they had had with the party for twenty-four years. Needless to say, it was a very difficult period for our party. For example, we were at the bottom of the polls, compound by the painful fact that almost three-quarters of the formers ministers in our government, who were natural SLPP diehards, had abandoned us (D. Harris, 2011; M. Wundah, 2009, 2004, 2012).

My appointment was deemed a blessing in disguise, considering the fact that our party was not only behind in the opinion polls, it had also become unpopular by the time the Cold War came to an end. Most of those who were now left at the helm of the party, especially those who had served in previous cabinets, were extremely unpopular.

Luckily, some of us had not served in the cabinet throughout. In my position as secretary general, I was one of the few members who was still credible to carry the party through. The other credible ones included Victor Foh, Pa Liverse, S. A. T. Koroma, F. B. Turay, Brima

O'Tole, Pa Shears, Sorsoh Conteh, M. L. Bangura, and Nancy Steele (A. Bundu, 2005; J. L. Hirsch, 2001).

I must confess that my relationship with President Momoh was not cordial. If it had been his choice, he wouldn't have offered me the post of secretary general. I was only offered the position because I was one of the few credible members of the APC.

I have cordial working relationships with most people. It is one of the strongest aspects of my social and interpersonal skills, which I acquired when I was in England and the Caribbean. I rarely despise anyone, but, sincerely speaking, President Momoh was not my cup of tea.

However, I didn't hate him, and never once did I attempt to betray his trust, even though there was none. And with time, I came to realise that he didn't like me either. Whenever we were together (which was very seldom), I could sense a feeling of mutual resentment. Whenever I asked for an appointment to see him, he was never spontaneous; he always asked me to come back at a later time.

I pondered over the situation and realised that I had to work with him for the progress of our party. I sought a solution, an arbitrator, an interlocutor, or peacemaker between me and the president. J. B. Dauda (alias Jam Body), was one of the president's best friends. Dauda hails from the eastern region of the country, one of the traditional strongholds of the SLPP, our main political rivals.

Dauda was appointed one of the most senior cabinet ministers in Momoh's government, which was a strategic move. Dauda was deemed a unifier who had the potential to build the APC Party and galvanise support for it in that part of the country. Besides, the president had personal liking for him.

So, I appealed to him to be the peacemaker for the president and me, the go-between. It was planned professionally. I would tell Dauda anything I needed as secretary general for the attention of the president as leader of the party.

It was a herculean task. We were still poles apart; all the same, I carried on with my job. The most important task, I reckoned, was to renew the fortunes of our party and bring back those who had disserted us. Above all, the party is more than any leader. Leaders come and go, but the party stays; it is capable of surviving all the storms. Despite these short-comings, I set the party in readiness for the pending elections in 1992.

The success of any political party depends on those who manage the operational machinery. I may have had problems with the party leadership, in the person of J. S. Momoh. However, I put together a functional and formidable party secretariat staff for the battle at hand. At the party secretariat, I had the veteran journalist I. B. Kargbo as information secretary, Filie Faboy as assistant general secretary, and a host of young and articulate men to man the fort.

Within a month, the tide began to change from gloomy to one of relative success. The signs were good; we began to attract more voters. Our publicity machinery was potent. Above all, our message was concise and honest. My team was new, never involved in political bigotry, never involved in corruption. My team and I put up strong, logical, and honest arguments. We did not deny we were the APC, but we were a "New Brand of APC."

Members of other parties were masquerading as saints, but I damned their claims as profane and sacrilege. Whenever impropriety was levied against the APC, I would argue as follows: "Yes, that was the case, but it was not an exclusively indigenous APC per se. It was a mixture of all political parties, including former senior cabinet ministers of the SLPP. They may argue that they were constrained by legislation to join the APC, but that didn't justify the fact that they indulged in corruption and corrupt practices.

"One of the senior ministers," I continued, "even became a vice president, and some were ministers or deputy ministers under the APC one-party regime. It was easy to conclude that these forced politicians were there only to serve the interest of their dissolved political parties, and that whenever multi-party democracy was restored, they would resuscitate their parties. In brief, they were political wolves in sheep clothing."[71]

Returning to the issue of the 1991 constitution, I am proud to reveal that I was a member of the Constitutional Review Committee. I played my part to help restore democracy in Sierra Leone. This measure of service to my country was done in good faith and emphasises the fact that country comes first before political parties of any persuasion.

I must pay homage to the late Bambay Kamara (former commissioner of police). When the APC was left destitute and confused, in the midst of this chaos, he and others who had the love of the party at heart prevailed on me to lead the APC.

With the advent in full throttle of political pluralism, the University of Sierra Leone invited all political party leaders to a debate at the university campus. President Momoh categorically refused to attend, likewise Dr Abdulai Conteh, his vice president; the buck was passed on to me and Mr Victor Foh.

A date was set, and I was more than willing to appear on behalf of the discredited APC Party. I knew from the onset that I had no dry bones in my closet; I was clean, politically speaking. I had never served in any ministerial position or as a director. During all this period, I was only a solitary back bencher in Parliament and then secretary general of the party.

The debate was scheduled to begin at 8 pm. I decided to appear late. I wanted the other political party leaders to occupy their seats and kick-start the debate before I rolled in. I wanted to see the reaction of the audience when I entered the auditorium. I knew I would attract catcalls, boos, and so on—and that was exactly what I needed to be energised.

I entered the auditorium after the two leaders had already spoken. I was dressed in a white suit with a large red square in my breast pocket and a white hanky in my hand. The expected boos came spontaneously. Reflecting on the decades of the mismanagement by the "Old APC," one can't blame them. Thus, I didn't begrudge them for their reaction towards me. They shouted, "APC, APC, rogue and crooked party, go back home and rust; you have nothing to tell us."

In response, I clapped my hands and gave them the broadest smile I ever exhibited in my life. Then I took my seat on the top table. I briefly noted with satisfaction that there was only one leader there who was not a senior member of the ruling APC Party: Joe Conteh of the United National People's Party (UNPP).

The rest, including Sallia Jusu Sheriff (SLPP), Thaimu Bangura (PDP), Edward Kargbo (PNP), and John Karimu (NUP), had served the party as cabinet ministers or in other capacities. Especially, I noted that the four main party leaders—Sheriff, Bangura, Kargbo, and Hassan Gbessay Kanu—were all key players in the APC administration. They held hefty positions in the one-party administration.

When it was my turn and I was invited to make my presentation, the boos and catcalls went on for almost ten minutes. Instead of allowing them to continue to scorn me, I injected humour as a counter-measure, neutralising them. As the crowd kept booing, I clapped as well as booed them. Even when they stopped booing, I continued, entreating them to tire so soon. My humour paid off.

I adamantly continued to boo them, and they literally begged me to take the stage and do my presentation. Before I made my statement, I sought my fundamental right to be heard, a basic norm of democratic rule.

I started my speech by acknowledging the failures of the APC in many areas of governance. "These failures," I said, "were the collective responsibilities of 90 percent of those panellists sitting right in front of you." I said, among other things, "My humble self, a back bencher in Parliament, was marginalised by the leadership of the APC for the past years, only to be called to clear the mess for them."

I posed the question, "Are you going to punish me for their mismanagement of the state? I come to ignite a new path for this country. Please join the new, clean, unblemished leadership of the New Sierra Leone under the APC Party." To support my arguments, I submitted the following facts to the audience:

1) I said all these leaders were collectively responsible for the bad policies made under the one-party rule.
2) They never resigned from the government when they were cabinet ministers; they were now accusing the APC government of corruption. Why didn't they resign?
3) They left the APC (good riddance) and formed their own political parties as a mark of selfishness.

I asked the audience whether they would believe those who sat at the high table, the proverbial old wine mixed with pure new wine. The answer was loud and clear: "No, no, no."

I appealed to the audience to look at the facts critically and give the verdict as they saw it.

In my final submission, I said, "You have to join me so that together, I can clean up the politics of this country. It is our country we are talking about, so let us bury our differences. These gentlemen, these wolves dressed in sheep clothing, have all failed you and this nation in the past. You are too intelligent to be fooled once more and join hands with them.

"I implore you, don't you ever listen to their empty promises. They have no future for this country. With your blessings, the future of this, our great and beloved country, Sierra Leone, rests in our hands. Together, we can turn a new page. As from today, let us vow together that we shall honour and practice accountability, transparency, all the values of good governance under the banner of our 1991 constitution, of which drafting committee I was a proud member."[72]

I must state that at the end of that debate, I was proud that there was renewed hope for the future of our party, the New APC, and above all our country. I left the auditorium accompanied by resounding applause from all and sundry. This experience emboldened me further to pursue my political career, no matter whatever challenges were put in my way.

H.E Ambassador Edward M. Turay With Queen Elizabeth 11

H.E Ambassador Edward. M. Turay With President Karlos Papoulias Of Greece On The Presentation Of Credentials In Greece

H.E Ambassador Edward M. Turay With President Karolos Papoulias On The Presentation Of Credentials In Greece

H.E Ambassador Edward M. Turay
In Discussion With President Mary Mcaleese of The Republic Of Ireland

Presentation In Republic Of Ireland

H.E Ambassador Edward .M.turay Inspecting A Guard Of Honour
By The Military With The President Of The Republic Of Ireland

Portugal: H.E Ambassador Edward M. Turay Seen With President Anibal Cavaco Silver

H.E Ambassador .Edward M. Turay Inspecting A Guard Of Honour In Portugal

H.E Ambassador Edward M. Turay on his way to present his credentials to Her Majesty Queen Elizabeth II, at Buckingham Palace.

CHAPTER 10

GATHERING THE POLITICAL MOMENTUM

"We face neither east, nor west: we face forward."

Kwame Nkrumah

It was apparent that the whole nation was sitting on tenterhooks. There was a knife-edge desire to actualise change at all cost. Politically, I was growing in confidence. Like the feelings of the country, I had promised myself that come what may, there was no turning back. I was facing neither east nor west, all I faced was forward. The debate at FBC had its effects nationally, especially among the middle ranks and the level-headed grassroots.

As stated inter alia, I had taken up the most important post of national secretary general at a time when our party was flat on its back. Not only that, to retaliate, I had not been the choice of the late President Momoh. However, destiny was on my side. The large majority of the rank and file of the party members agreed that I would be the ideal choice for this position.

I hadn't had any ministerial experience, nor had I held any position in the party before. I was a bit apprehensive to take the offer, but not due to these facts; after all, I had solid professional experience and an immense quality of education and qualifications, which many in the party hierarchy hadn't. Not only that, the divisive factional culture had gained dangerous roots.

It was an open secret among the elite of the party. Members of the Binkolo diaspora did not particularly like me, so I emphatically refused to accept the offer. Not only that, deep in my heart, I considered the offer a ploy, and a very opportunistic one at that. My instincts told me that some of those who would drive the dagger and twist it in me had decided to use this ploy. Their ulterior motive: They were determined to see me fail; now our great party had gone to the dogs. In her heyday, they wouldn't let someone like me whisper interest, let alone declare or apply for the job of leader of the party.

I must reveal that even at the time when our party was at its lowest ebb in the opinion polls, we were not short of generous, committed, and considerate personalities. Against all the odds, there were truly committed people in the hierarchy who would sacrifice all they had acquired for the benefit of the party.

One of these people was Bambay Kamara. He was commissioner of police (the modern equivalent of inspector general of police). He was the nation's only expert in fingerprint analysis. As a great and successful senior detective, he had set up a functional CID, against all the odds.

He was also a great sports fanatic, especially for football. With his own personal finance, Kamara had transformed the Edwards Football Club into a one of the most formidable and successful teams in the country. He was also a passionate politician, and so he stepped in.

After persistent pleas from Kamara,[73] the youths, and the women's wing of the party, they won the day. I agreed to accept the position. I took over the position at the end of 1991. In addition to their personal pleas, I accepted the offer in order to go down in history as the rescuer of the party when it all went wrong.

My preliminary tasks, and urgent ones at that, were to restructure the party and make it functional and relevant once more. The party had lost credibility, and the leadership was despised by the electorate. So the task to reorganise the secretariat was huge. With an organised, well-structured party secretariat, we would be well placed to embark on holistic reforms. The other formidable challenge we faced was beefing up the finances of the party, which had dried up. The party was bankrupt.

Again, the reality had dawned on the reasonable members of the party hierarchy that the vessel needed a new captain, a new party secretary. There was, however, lingering recalcitrance. Those who belonged to this backward and un-progressive camp had a motive: to frustrate our efforts and undermine every effort we made at the secretariat.

One of the recalcitrant forces was the former secretary general of the party; he was determined to go under my skin and render me and my team ineffective. A member of the Binkolo diaspora, he and his co-conspirators had made their disapproval of me as national secretary general an open secret.

There is nowhere in world, including the Western industrialised world, where one could organise and rejuvenate a political party without a lot of capital. In Sierra Leone, as well as elsewhere in Africa, there is nothing like political party funding schemes. We don't enjoy the kind of financial luxuries which Western political parties enjoy, by way of massive fundraising by corporations and millionaires. Hence, my next headache was how to fund my structural reforms and organisation.

To reiterate, Bambay Kamara was not only a party faithful, he was a nice human being, generous and very caring. I called on him anytime I needed money to run the secretariat. In my view, this was a deliberate act: to starve me financially so as to make me look incompetent and incapable as national secretary general. It was a heavy-handed strategy and came from above, as I was made to understand. There was even more to the sabotage. I was regarded as an outsider and should not be allowed to operate the party's accounts.

A great rescuer came to my aid when I was in dire need. Miraculously, he sent in a team of formidable, tenacious, intelligent, efficient, and committed rescuers. Together, these gentlemen and I turned the fortunes of the party around.

The team included Kargbo, the veteran journalist and mouthpiece of the party, very popular nationally and internationally; Faboy, the assistant secretary general, uniquely subservient and always ready to do what he was told; and Juxton Smith (the new resident minister, East), a great man and deeply committed to the APC course. They galvanised the help of others, and like in the early decades of the party, we started to have hands on deck in order to rejuvenate the APC.

The above appointments were strategic and crucial to the aspirations of the party. In the good old days, during the era of Siaka Stevens, the party grassroots had loyalists in the Kono District, Eastern Region of Sierra Leone. Hence, Fabio's[74] appointment as the deputy secretary general was a strategy to win votes in the future. Also, it was a sound effort to unify the country and dispel all the misgivings which regional and ethnic divisions had brought to bear on us.

Kargbo's pedigree as one of the most capable journalists in the country added a feather in the cap of the party. With such a figure as the public orator and media guru of the party, we were on course to hammer home our new message and woo the electorate once more.

In addition to all the restructuring issues and fundraising needs, time was not on our side. The 1992 General Elections were looming large. I drew up a plan for the pending campaign. In addition, I drew up a list of unquestionably loyal members from the youths, women, and student wings of the party.

Now, we had a comprehensive list of planning strategies. Strategy one was rebranding the party. It had gone into the gutters, so we had first all to make it likeable and attractive once more.

Thus, I wrote the following memo to my comrades at the secretariat and reform-minded senior officials and the young generation of the party:

"We all do realise that our party has become a spent force. We must put all behind us, be optimistic and reform this Great Party of ours. We have a lot to do in order to achieve this goal. First we must start by embarking on the formidable task of rebranding and re-inventing the party for the consumption of the electorate."

My vision and message, as I clearly stated during the debate at FBC, was simple. As the new national secretary general of the APC, I must be seen as part and parcel of the new brand. I rebranded it as the "New APC Party,: with a new vision, a new focus, and a new sense of purpose. The old, outgoing APC was a conglomerate of old political parties forced by law to dissolve and constitute themselves under the one-party system of government, introduced by the late Siaka Stevens.

In all my arguments and at discussions panels, I hammered home these pertinent points. I had to reiterate the points. The essence was to have their desired effects on the minds of the populace. None of the Old Guards had genuine allegiance to the APC Party (even though some of them were given senior cabinet positions, and one became vice president).

The APC one-party government, in my view, was a disaster, in the sense that some of these politicians only joined the party by force of the law (i.e., the new constitution brought about the one-party system). They also needed the system as a source of survival; they had no love for the APC Party per se. In fact, they wanted the one-party system of government to fail.

I was not creating a political caricature of the system; rather, I painted the true picture as it was. Thus, the reactions of President J. S. Momoh to the enduring system he inherited justify my assertions. The APC became so hated and unpopular that President Momoh declared a return to democratic pluralism.

It was on this basis that the president appointed a committee to look into the Constitution, with a view to returning the country to democracy. I was a member of this committee, which unanimously recommended the adoption of the 1991 Constitution, which was overwhelmingly passed in Parliament.

After the 1991 Constitution went through Parliament, the one-party APC government was completely disintegrated. The old established parties re-organised themselves, the SLPP resurfaced, and new political parties were formed, including the Peoples' Democratic Party (led by Thaimu Bangura), the United National Peoples' Party (led by Kerefa Smart), and the National Unity Party (led by John Karimu).[75]

I must state with pride that due to the reforms injected into the party by me and my team at the secretariat, we were truly up and running for the 1992 elections. Our campaign had great momentum. I led the campaign with the help of the secretariat. Amazingly, the leadership of President Momoh and his henchmen didn't give the secretariat any realistic support, financially or morally.

Throughout our national campaigns, we emphasised the same message stated previously. Ours was a new brand, a reformed APC, with new ideas and a future for our country. To stick with the Old Guards[76] spelt nothing but backwardness and non-progressive political overtures. It would be disastrous for Sierra Leone as a nation, which we could not afford to risk.

The message was simple and direct. Throughout our politics since we attained independence, three vices have caused our backwardness, despite all our massive natural resources. The vices, I told my audience, were tribalism, nepotism, and corruption. I sustained the argument that the very politicians of the Old Guard who were masquerading as trusted and reformed politicians were the architects of these vices. As the campaigns went on, the calculation of the secretariat was that the message was well received with the electorate, and the scale of support was beginning to rise, especially in the Western area, where we thought we had a wider understanding of issues raised by all political parties.

CHAPTER 11

THE NPRC MILITARY INTERVENTION

"Power attained by violence is tantamount to defeat, for it is momentary."

Mahatma Gandhi (paraphrased; 1869-1948)

That Sierra Leoneans were eager for democratic renewal is an understatement. We are a generous and peace-loving nation. Political disruption had been imposed on us as a nation. The whole country was waiting eagerly to go back to the drawing board and make lasting amends. The 1992 General Elections were envisioned as historical, the nation's date with destiny.

Unfortunately, it wasn't meant to be. The democracy we were preparing for was interrupted at a time when Sierra Leoneans were eager to clean up politics and reinvent the good image of the country. At this time, the military struck, marking the beginning of hubris.

The military junta that overthrew President Momoh was known as the National Provisional Redemption Council (NPRC). Being the tradition of all military juntas, when they seized power, the NPRC suspended the national constitution, and civil institutions were dissolved.

The political leaders were ordered to give themselves up to the police for their own safety. By this time, President Momoh had already fled to Guinea. This was then followed by an array of mass arrests of cabinet ministers, politicians, and supporters; they were sent to the Pademba Road Maximum-Security Prison.

I had no trust in the military brass, who were young and unstable and greedy. I hid for some days in the Congo Cross area of Freetown. Somehow, a group of young soldiers found my hiding place and demanded my surrender, or else they would kill me and everyone in the house. I therefore gave myself up; I was immediately arrested and taken to the Congo Cross Police Station.

A few hours later, the same group of soldiers came to the police station and demanded my release. The officer in charge refused to let me go until the most senior officer in the group signed a release document—which was done instantly. I was then taken from the station and led towards Brookfields, via St. Johns Roundabout. The vehicle headed for Sanders Street, but there were a lot of people blocking the way.

At that point, the driver had no choice but to divert to Campbell Street and Pademba Road. Even there, there was a large crowd of people. We headed towards Circular Road. As we drove along, the soldiers were shouting and saying, "We have arrested Eddie Turay, Secretary General of the APC Party, and we are taking him to Kissy Ferry terminal to join his political colleagues."

After taking the curve at the junction of Circular Road and Berry Street, leading to Fourah Bay College, there was a huge crowd of students. They rushed in front of our vehicle, demanding that I be returned to Pademba Road Prison. I could hear distinctly students shouting my name, saying, "Oh no, Eddie Turay is clean, innocent, and has just joined the APC Party a few months ago—let him go."

Not only that, as they kept shouting for my release and proclaiming my innocence, Dr Gebril, a military doctor, came to the scene. Being a senior officer of the military junta, he ordered the soldiers to take me to Pademba Road Prison.

In fact, he ordered the young soldiers to transfer me to his vehicle, which they did, and he drove me to Pademba Road Prison safely. As I was handed over to the prison authority, I saw a few guards I knew before, when they used to attend court with prisoners and attend to other court-related matters.

They sympathised with my situation. They were very kind to me, and now and again, they tried to calm me down and gave me hope and courage.

I was lodged at Clarkson House, in cell # 10.[77]

The cell was about ten feet by ten feet, with a vent at the top. It had the most deplorable sanitation and hygienic conditions. The precarious situation was similar to deteriorating from grace to filthy grass.

I tried to make sense out of the situation and put myself together. It was then that it dawned on me that I must face reality. The reality was that law and order had broken down in a country we held to our hearts. I suppressed my tears and said to myself, *You are in a cell, your country is on the brink; there is no place for tears, so be a man and have faith in the Lord.*

As I looked around, I noticed some writings on the wall. I looked closely and carefully; what I saw brought me huge hope and confidence that I would not stay long in this place.

The words on the wall were simple. They said:

"It is better to trust in the Lord than trust in Man."

All of a sudden, I experienced a surge in my spirit and heard myself crying to God, saying, *"Please, God, forgive me for everything I have done in my life, and have mercy on me."*

It felt as if the walls of Pademba Road Prison were beginning to melt gradually and that freedom was in sight.

I cried bitterly. And then I began to take stock of my personal life style. I had lived a life of a "lover boy": young, educated, and articulate. I was the youngest magistrate in the Sierra Leone Judiciary and a highly successful criminal lawyer. In politics, I became secretary general of the ruling APC Party. Added to all these accolades, I was a member of Parliament of one the most successful and oldest political parties in Sierra Leone, if not in Africa.

Overwhelmed by this string of successes, I became pompous and full of youthful indiscretion. Due to my past rollercoaster records, I thought God had no place in my life. I pleaded to God, saying that I had just assumed the position of secretary general of the APC ruling party, four months ago.

Despite my checkered history in the other areas mentioned above, one thing stood out: I had never been a cabinet minister or was involved in corruption, nepotism, or tribalism. With regards to these, I was innocent; so confidently, and touched by the Spirit of His Grace, I asked God to set me free from this place.

I prayed the whole evening and felt a spiritual connection with God, which made me more relaxed and confident in my new location, the prison.

My first night in prison changed my perception of life. At one point, I said to myself, *A man is as good as dead, since my predicament has decided to leave my lot and I empty vessels.*[78]

After hours, I thought otherwise. In all you do and think, always call on the name of the Lord. I prayed, cried, and pleaded with God to forgive me, and He did just that.

Four days later, I was the first inmate to be released by the junta. The following Sunday, I rushed to Jesus Is Lord Ministry and surrendered my life to Jesus Christ as my Lord and Saviour.

After only a week of freedom, subversive leaflets surfaced in the streets of Freetown; these leaflets, captioned "Lord Da Mercy,"[79] were very critical of the junta. Everything done by the junta was carried negatively by these leaflets.

The junta thought (wrongfully) that I was behind these leaflets; I was again arrested and detained at Pademba Road Prison. It was my second innings, but even at that, I spent only four days in prison and was released.

I have never doubted the fact that whenever I am faced with difficulties, the memories of my late father virtually haunt me. Once, when I was a pupil at Our Lady of Fatima, advised me:

"Eddie, always bear in my mind after the God your serve and I, your father, you have one reliable friend. That friend is education; it never fails, it is a dependable asset."[80]

I had been prepared well enough, so I had something concrete I could fall back on, in case of any mishap. I went back to my legal practice. Here in court, I would work with peace of mind. Anyway, returning to my practice didn't make me a political renegade.

One day, I was in court when a journalist interviewed me about the fate of the APC Party. I told this journalist that whether the junta liked it or not, the "APC is coming back." That single statement was used against me. It was all over the newspapers the next morning. I was arrested for the third time and sent to Pademba Road Prison.

This time around, I was kept in a cell for three weeks. During this time in prison, agents of the junta torched my house at Marjay Town. At the time, no one was in the house; my children were at school, and I was in prison. Neighbours saw a military Landover parked in front of my house, and suddenly the house was on fire, and they drove off.

I was released the next day. I came home to find out I had lost everything. As an interim measure, I was offered accommodations by Mrs Formeh Kamara, at Brookfields. I received donations of clothing, cooking utensils, and food from good friends and relatives.

Two weeks later, I was arrested for the fourth time on the flimsy grounds that I had been linked with a plot to over-throw the junta. I was sent again to Pademba Road Prison.

By this time, I was full of joy and happiness in the name of Jesus Christ. Fear was no longer my portion. I harboured no hatred for the junta boys; neither was I afraid of them, nor did I ever respect them.

I was rearrested and detained at Pademba Road Prison six more times, until Claude Campbell, a trusted friend, intervened and threatened to resign as the junta's attorney general unless the arrests stopped or charges were entered against me. Eventually, the arrests stopped completely.

My last and final release from prison was a divine manifestation of God's plan for His people. One Friday afternoon, a guard came to my cell and said to me nervously, "Eddie, you are released—go home."[81]

I said, "What? What did you say?"

He repeated, "You have been released by the junta, go home."

I packed up whatever belongings I had and went home; it was around six o'clock.

When my family saw me, they thought I had escaped. Tired but very happy, I washed and went to bed after loudly praising my Lord.

I did not wake until about one o'clock in the afternoon the next day. I noticed a large crowd standing opposite my balcony. When they saw me, every one of them ran away from me. I was amazed and wondered what was wrong. Later, my son came in and told me what happened the day I left prison.

117

According to my son, on that Friday midnight, a group of NPRC soldiers came to the prison and removed, at gun point, the other twenty-four inmates I left in residence when I was released. They were all shot and disposed of by the junta.[82]

I was overwhelmed by joy. I just praised God for what He had done for me. He located me and fished me out in the last minute.

My experiences since the NPRC Junta took power reminded of one salient fact. God can step in at the last second for anyone, and what He did in my case is a classic example. These experiences and the miraculously manner in which I was rescued by God galvanised my faith. Undoubtedly, the Lord helps all and sundry, if only you trust Him in faith and in truth.

I later learned that the crowd that fled when they saw me on the balcony thought I was a ghost; they came to render a vigil in memory of me.

During the course of the day, a lot of people called to see me at home.

One of the callers was a military officer, an in-law of mine. He said, "Eddie, when I learnt about the plan to execute all the political leaders in prison, I sent word to a common friend of ours to call all the Muslims in the area to pray for you throughout Friday night." He never disclosed the reason for the prayers. They knew I was in prison and needed prayers for God's intervention.

I say to all who read this book, what God has done for me, He can do for you if you only believe. God said quite clearly to mankind, His creation, to the whites, the blacks, the reds, the pales, and the pinks, that before each one of us was born, He knew us. He has destined, ordained, and planned for us in this world. If the Lord rescued me out of the jaws of death, He can do it for you, if you are ever in similar situation — if only you believe!

CHAPTER 12

THE HISTORIC BINTUMANI CONFERENCE

⌒◦⌒

"Strength does not come from physical capacity. It comes from an indomitable will."

Mahatma Gandhi

The stage that was created at the Historic Bintumani Conference Hall signified the contrast between David and Goliath in terms of differences in strength. But for sheer will power, determination, and resoluteness, the military would have won the day. The civic representatives from all walks of life manifested an indomitable will to have their say heard (A. T. Kabbah, 2010; D. Harris, 2011; J. L. Hirsch, 2001).

The military had spent only four and a half years in power, yet it became very unpopular. Historically, the country they had imposed themselves on were neither accustomed to nor an admirer of military rule. The last time the nation had a military regime was in 1967, during the military coup and countercoup of brigadiers David Lansana and Juxton Smith (S. P. Riley, 1996; A. K. Koroma, 1996; J. A. D. Alie, 2007).

Since then, the country enjoyed relative peace and tranquillity, especially under President Siaka Stevens. Those intermittent attempted coups were met by waves of contempt and national disapproval. Hence, the country hadn't any more appetite for any form of military rule, even if it included a mixture of politicians and civilians from various walks of life.

People have argued elsewhere that the advent of the NPRC was greeted by overwhelming joy and nationwide acceptance. Well, the reasons were not farfetched. For decades, the one-party system of government had squeezed the nation and left them extremely disillusioned. Therefore, any measure adopted to oust what became an extremely unpopular civilian regime would have been acceptable.

In total, whether short lived in office or not, instrument of an early euphoric-oriented politics or whatever, the NPRC military junta had outweighed its usefulness. By way of reaction, enormous pressure was mounted on its members to hand over power to a democratically elected civilian government. The same demand resonated in the international community. There were calls from every corner of the world for the resignation of the government and the conduction of elections earlier than later.

The junta was determined to stay in power; they decided to play high politics, so they devised a way to hand over power and called a conference of all political parties and other stake-holders. In reality it was a ploy at best; not in a million years did they want to relinquish the throne and bring a credible democratic renewal. The conference was held at one of the most popular landmarks in the country, the historic Bintumani Hotel. The idea was to present two options:[83]

(1) Elections now before peace.
(2) Attain peace first before elections.

The first conference was dubbed Bintumani One. Each political party was given a chance to address the conference and convey their position.

I was then the de-facto secretary general of the APC Party, and the lot fell on me to deliver the position of my party on the General Election debate. The secretariat wrote a speech for me to deliver; by then, I had grown in the Lord, and I asked God to speak through me.

When I was called to deliver my address, I again asked the Lord to speak through me (referring to 2 Corinthians 10:12, which warns that "comparing themselves among themselves is not wise") I accused the junta of comparing the APC government's handling of the war as negligible as opposed to their prosecution of the same war.

It was dishonest to accuse President J. S. Momoh of complacency in the prosecution of the war. The president or any other person in power could only utilise the military resources at their disposal to fight the war. There is a sound adage that says, "You can't give what you don't have."

On the podium, I perceived them differently in their resplendent uniforms, bloated and self-promoted, and portrayed the faces of the devil incarnate. I meditated in my heart and implored the Lord to speak through me.

In my speech, I outlined the keys points they needed to consider to make an informed judgment. It went like this:[84]

"Ladies and gentlemen, gallant soldiers of the NPRC, and members of the diplomatic and consular corps.

"You recall when the APC government was in power, fighting this war, through the state military power, the Junta accused the said government of not providing enough military resources to fight the war and win it; the reason why you took over power was to end the war. You also accused the APC government of corruption. Now, you are in control, my young gallant soldiers, fighting the war which the APC government failed to do. I ask you this question: where was the war on the day you took power from the APC government?"

As I was speaking, I could sense the feeling of the audience and the gnashing of teeth by the military men. I said, "I will tell you where the war was on the day you took over power from us. I dare say, the war that the APC government fought so gallantly was behind the Mano River Bridge on the Liberian side, but today, as you sit here pompously, the war has expanded and gone beyond Mano River Bridge. It is between Hastings and Freetown, and rapidly advancing to the heart of the city. Can you imagine that?"

I paused for a second so that the realities would sink in and take control of their imagination and sense of judgment. Then I turned to the military brass at the high table, the high command, including their leader, and boldly told them in a defiant tone, "You are soldiers, not politicians. You enlisted in the Sierra Leone Armed Forces in order to defend this nation. Pack your kits and go back to your barracks."

I exposed their flaws to their face. I mimicked them: "Gallant soldiers of this great realm, give me your stubborn ears for once! Since you ousted the democratically elected government of this nation, you have been parading around as the so-called saviours. You not only contemptuously slapped the serene, golden word 'patriotism' in the face, you made a mockery of it. How? You claimed to be patriotic, but you have taken this country down the gutters. Shame on you! I want to point out to you that on both counts as in all other counts of your flimsy promises, you have failed this nation woefully." Then I posed this challenge: "If you believe you are as popular as you and your cronies think, then I challenge you. Dissolve your regime, retreat to the barracks where you belong, and call immediate elections."

There was a resounding round of applause, followed by spontaneous, chaotic pandemonium around the conference arena. The crowd booed the military brass and hurled insults on them. The meeting came to an end without any conclusion, as the junta left the hall surreptitiously. Personally, I breathed a huge sigh of relief and summoned renewed confidence in the rejuvenation of our party.

As I was leaving the hall, Nigeria's High Commissioner, H.E. Alhaji Abu-Bakarr, said to me that he admired my courage and admonished me to be careful. Not only that, he went a step further and said on a serious note. "If you were in Nigeria, it would have been a different case."[86]

A shiver ran down my spine as I pondered the danger I was in. I was never in the good books of the NPRC Junta. After they toppled the administration of President J. S. Momoh, I had been their key target.

On many occasions, I had narrowly escaped death in their hands; to boldly castigate them, tell them the truth in the presence of the entire nation, foreign diplomats, and the world media was the last straw that broke the camel's back.

I rushed to my office downtown, where I was greeted by a large crowd of supporters waiting for me. A word came from the Jesus Is Lord Ministry that while I was giving my speech, prayers for the Lord's protection were being said on my behalf.

At the same time, I was made to understand that the international community rushed to admonish the junta on the fluid situation. That is, if any harm was done to me, the world would hold them accountable.

I was a bit relieved that members of the foreign diplomatic community were solidly behind me for the brave stance I took against the junta in defence of democracy. Later, the German charge d'affaires called to assure me of the support of the international community, adding that the diplomatic community had warned the junta to stay clear from me. Any violence against me would render them answerable to the international community.

As the day wore on, it became apparent that against all the odds, democracy would eventually win the day in our beloved Sierra Leone.

And that brought me to another one of my dad's sayings:

"In all that you do in life, my son, be loyal and steadfast to the truth. It is only the truth that shall set you free. Have no fear, seek no favours, no matter how flamboyant they might be, in exchange for defending the ethics of the truth. Don't betray the truth, or else you betray your soul."[87]

The junta had smelt the rat; it was only trying to play delay tactics. It had realised that the people were ready to take back that which genuinely belonged to them. The junta realised that the people were determined to turn back the hands of the clock; they were ready to rewrite history.

Above all, since independence in 1961, the people realised that they had either been cowed into mortgaging their rights or bereft of it through empty promises. The time had come for them to take back power for the common good. In the chaotic climate of the inclusive conference, the populace resolved. By resolution, all the political parties and other stake-holders of the dream for democratic renewal agreed to conduct elections before peace.

CHAPTER 13

THE 1996 ELECTIONS

———◁◉▷———

"Faith is taking the first step, even when you don't see
the whole staircase."

Dr Martin Luther King Jr.

Sierra Leone regained independence on 27 April 1961, with Her
Majesty the Queen as the head of state. Sir Milton Margai of the
Sierra Leone People's Party (SLPP) was the country's first prime
minister, followed by Sir Albert Margai, and then in 1968, Siaka
Stevens of the APC became prime minister (S. E. Berewa, 2011).

The abortive coup of 1971 emboldened Stevens to declare Sierra
Leone a republic; he made sweeping constitutional changes that
culminated in the enactment of the 1978 Republican Constitution,
which effectively made Sierra Leone a one-party republican state, with
Stevens its first president.

Stevens survived many coup attempts. In 1986, he arbitrarily handed
over power to Joseph Saidu Momoh. The year 1992 saw the removal
of Momoh from power by young army officers, led by Captain
Valentine Strasser. Under the National Provisional Ruling Council

(NPRC), elections were slated for 1996 for a peaceful return to civilian rule (S. E. Berewa, 2011; J. A. D. Alie, 1990; D. Harris, 2011).

It was the most trying period of our party. But as stated above, faith means taking steps, even if it means leaping into the dark. As the 1996 elections approached, the University of Sierra Leone's Fourah Bay College scheduled debates by all political parties contesting the elections.

As was to be expected, the APC Party was the underdog; they were very unpopular and had been deserted by many of its key members to form their own political parties.

The deposed president, J. S. Momoh, was in the neighbouring Republic of Guinea. I went to seek his advice and ask about the viability of APC entering the race. He categorically advised against it, on the premise that the junta would never allow them to take part in the elections. He cited some secret information he had received from the junta.

However, on my return to Freetown, the remnants, especially the faithful of the party, decided to participate. The logic was sound, at least to register our presence and have it recorded in history that the APC was once a great party in Sierra Leone.

Most of us were in favour of APC contesting the elections on that sound premise. It is sad all of those who favoured this important premise have died. I dedicate this book to their memories, for the great service they rendered to our party and country: Nancy Steele, Dondodo Tomgbeh Tomgbeh, Ya Alimamy, and a host of others. The elections were to be conducted under the new constitution.

The 1996 General Elections added another feather to my cap. The prophecies of my father were gradually gathering pace with every passing moment of our national politics. I must reiterate that according to the internal factions of our party, I was deemed one of the outsiders. The gurus and Old Guards, that is, those who held ministerial positions in the party, nurtured the same perception, even during the regime of President J. S. Momoh.[88]

When it was all a bed of roses, not a single time was I exposed to the opportunities that the crème de la crème enjoyed. I was not part of it; I say this not with contempt or any form of malice for the two late leaders, but because of inherent situations beyond their control.

In politics, horse trading (sacrificing people for strategic political gains) is a common phenomena. Collectively, it is important to consider these political realities and their wider ramifications for the survival of the party. The safety of the party, they say, is greater than the sum total of personal considerations and ambitions.

The APC, which had virtually gone out of circulation and was limping, was now showing concrete signs of recovery and revitalisation. We were now viable for re-elections, or at least for participation in the democratic process of our country.

We are one of the two main political parties in Sierra Leone. Prior to the chaotic periods narrated herein, we had ruled the longest, more than any political party in Sierra Leone, including our main rivals: the Sierra Leone People's Party.

The next major question was the choice of the APC presidential candidate. No one offered to contest. Maybe there was something these hitherto ambitious politicians knew, which I was not aware of. But should that be the case, where was I? Could I have been on Mars or Jupiter? It was an open secret that they virtually abandoned the idea to vie for the leadership of the party. Why? Deep in their heart of hearts, they were conscious of the fact that we wouldn't win.

I perceived this as immature and simplistic, to say the least. Why? Politics is about winning and losing. You can't afford to be blessed with any of these two contrasting scenarios; politics is like gambling: sometimes you win, sometimes you lose. The gods can't afford to favour you all the time. But the fact of the matter is that the Old Guards were used to winning, not the reverse.

I was still the national secretary general of the Party, a post I held since 1991. Amazingly, the lot fell on me to represent the APC in the contest as the flag bearer, the presidential candidate. As if I was inspired, I accepted the offer readily and chose Victor Foh as my running mate.

Foh deserved the position of running mate for many reasons. He had been loyal to the party, through thick and thin. His position was precarious. In the deep-seated regional and ethnic division of Sierra Leone's politics, Foh was a Mende and a southerner, a natural stakeholder and key strategist of the SLPP.

After all, politically speaking, one would have said without any shadow of doubt that the SLPP was his natural party. Yet, against all the odds, he had always stood by the party. He'd been intimidated by members of his natural constituency, yet Foh was an unshakable loyalist of the All People's Congress Party.

Having said that, it was simplistic to reckon that the APC would win, come what may; the view of the majority was that the APC would never win. And if by any miracle the APC won, the junta would never hand over power to us, for fear of reprisals. To be honest, no sane person in the country would believe the APC would ever win a seat, let alone the biggest of all stakes, the ace, the presidency.

Against the predictions of the sceptics, the party won five seats in Parliament. The winners were Victor Foh, Serry Kamal, Jenko Stevens, Filie Faboy, and I. Our small numerical strength in Parliament notwithstanding, we created a huge mark, because we had such high spirit. The SLPP, the majority party, followed by the UNPP and the PDP, respected us because of our quality contributions to parliamentary debates.

The 1996 elections are significant for many reasons. For example, it marked the end of the NPRC Junta. They had no choice, so they relinquished power to President Ahmed Tejan Kabbah of the SLPP. This period marked the return of multi-party democracy in Sierra Leone after almost three decades of one-party political dispensation (D. Harris, 2011; A. T. Kabbah, 2010).

It was now the advent of an SLPP government after decades in the political wilderness. The new government had a lot on its plate. First, they had to conclude the brutal civil war. In retrospect, ours had been a dysfunctional political dispensation, and the debris had affected societal cohesion. The corrosive issue, a malaise of corruption and patrimonial culture, had added to the dysfunction and the impact of the grotesque civil war.

Those are a summary of the painful headaches for anybody that would have ascended the throne in Sierra Leone at that time. For instance, the international community was determined to dispense justice by bringing culprits to book. The country itself had couched her own domestic schemes to dispense justice against war criminals. In summary, President Ahmed Tejan Kabbah had the herculean task of reconciling the fragmented nation he inherited.

It was a tough call for President Kabbah, to say the least. Not even in his days as senior member of the UN did he face such a difficult task. However, the ball was now in his court; he had no choice but get on with it. The good thing was that with the signing of the Lome Peace Accord in Lome, the Togolese capital, the signs were generally encouraging that after twelve years of a destructive civil war, members of the warring factions were prepared to make peace at last. But there were hiccups here and there.

I had a remarkable working relationship with Kabbah. I was chair of the Defence and Presidential Affairs Committee in Parliament. President Kabbah was a great man, sincere and honest in my view, but found himself a lamb in the SLPP den of wolves.

When he was president, I was the minority leader of the APC. As Parliament was settling down quite remarkably, on 25 May 1997, the military devils struck again. The so-called Armed Forces Redemption Council (AFRC) took power under the auspices of their leader, Johnny Paul Koroma. He was a renegade with clearly destructive intentions. Without wasting any time, he invited Foday Sankoh, the notorious RUF rebel leader, to join them (A. T. Kabbah, 2010, S E. Berewa, 2011, J L, Hirsch, 2001).

President Kabbah fled to Guinea, and I followed him later. We planned the perfect scheme and sold it off for the consumption of the AFRC Junta. This was how I did it. They were aware that the international community wouldn't recognise their regime. They planned a huge PR drive in order to improve their popularity and chances of acceptance by the international community.

Thus, an outfit of senior experts and professionals, including lawyers, were appointed to promote their interest on the global political scene. The person who led the delegation to the Nigerian head of state, Sunni Abacha, was Eke Halloway. They approached me to be part of the delegation. I saw it as the only opportunity to leave the country, so I accepted, and they fell for it.

On second thought, it was risky to travel with them. I made sure there was no space for errors. We were to travel in a helicopter to Conakry. I appealed to the junta to allow me to travel by road and join the rest of the delegation in Conakry. They let me go, after supplying me with enough gas, and instructed me to collect my allowance from the Sierra Leone ambassador in Conakry. I did not even visit the embassy. This was how I left Sierra Leone (after I had settled my family in a secured place somewhere in the north).

The nation was not aware of my plans. They thought I had betrayed the democratically elected government and joined the renegades. My name was all over the newspapers, saying that I had left the country to represent the junta on a mission to Nigeria. I didn't waste a single second to prove them wrong. On my arrival in Conakry, I called on President Tejan Kabbah to pledge my support to democracy and damned the AFRC.

I had to be swift, for it was a sensitive matter. I couldn't afford to implicate myself and betray the honour and integrity of my dead parents. Yes, I wanted political power, but not at all cost, especially not a strategy that cheats the values of democracy. I made my position clear by bringing in one of the oldest global mouthpieces of democracy and awareness—the BBC—in order to air my stance and clear any misinformation that was propagated by my critics.

The External Service had a rich, educative, and informative programme called "Focus on Africa." I phoned them and condemned the coup. Following that robust move, I then joined the other political parties to unequivocally demand an immediate handing over of power to the legitimate government of President Tejan Kabbah.

My mind was now at peace after all these concrete moves. The AFRC Junta was insulted and declared me a wanted refugee. Again, I have to personally thank the foreign diplomats then in Sierra Leone at this crucial period of our political history. They showed that they were in our country to drive home a very important message: the Cold War was over, so it was time for democratic pluralism.

The days of the military and renegades were truly over, so they could go all out to effectuate the tenets of the New World Order. The rationale was simple. It is incumbent on all to embrace and promote democracy for self-determination and empowerment. Members of the diplomatic community deemed it incumbent on all citizens of the world to embrace democracy and not to sabotage it.

In that context, I was warned while in the Republic of Guinea to be on my guard on arrival in Conakry. A Western diplomat told me, "You must watch your steps now that you have fled Sierra Leone. The junta has despatched a hit-squad to track you down and dispose of you."[89] I was perturbed. I went from one hiding place to the other, and finally I left for the United States as a refugee.

CHAPTER 14

The New Era Emerges

———◁●▷———

"The more extensive a man's knowledge of what has been done, the greater will be his power of knowing what to do."

Benjamin Disraeli (1804-1881)

I must confess that I was not very close to Ernest Bai Koroma when he was preparing to embark on his political career. However, I knew him very well as a young, dynamic businessman, with a string of business success. The president has admirable qualities. He is unassuming and behaves in a very gentlemanly manner at all times.

Regarding his features, President Koroma has such a huge presence; he is dignified and could attract anyone easily. He is very conscious and sensitive, with a mind of his own. Above all, he is very considerate. And when it comes to very serious matters, especially matters of state, he is flexible and compassionate but emphasises forthrightness in public office.

President Koroma is a very decent man who speaks guardedly, and one has to study his facial expression to know his personality well.

His smiles should not be taken for granted, for he treats issues with the utmost finesse. You can never catch him off guard. His sense of awareness is acute. He is always alert and extremely sensitive to the feelings of other people. He has a cynical smile; his white teeth are rarely seen out, which makes him seem like an intelligent and shrewd politician.[90]

My first one-to-one contact with him came about when I went to his office to solicit funds for the APC Party before the 1996 general elections.

When I was ushered into his office, he hurried to attend to me as soon as I entered. I was very much impressed by the sense of urgency he exhibited towards me. He gave me a decent amount of money, and I left.

Also, I reckoned one significant fact. He must have done extensive research and accumulated substantial knowledge about the past history of our great party for the benefits of future challenges. I realised this fact during the brief time I spent in his office and the sensible comments he made.

On my way out of his office, I noticed that plainclothes AFRC security men were lurking around, keeping watch on the entrance of the building. They were to keep account of his visitors, especially APC members. The military renegades' strategy was similar to the spook culture in the USSR during the Cold War.

With the passage of time, I realised that he was cautious due to the fact that he was apprehensive. Those were uncertain times; everyone was a watchdog for the regime. Thus, it was apparent that being a high-profile political figure, the regime was spying on him. And, to be honest, he couldn't afford to jeopardise his personal safety.

The second contact I had with President Koroma was in London. Little did I know that he was at my premises for an important reason. He visited me with Alpha Khan to disclose his intention to run for the leadership of the APC Party.

This was no longer the time for any party in-fighting. Rather, I believed that it was time to unify our great party. Without any reservations, I congratulated him and confirmed to him his inalienable right to contest for the presidency under the APC banner. Again, he was very magnanimous in his approach towards me and the matter. The leadership qualities could be seen oozing from his gentle smile and entire body language.

My exile in the United States reminded me of some of our former African political leaders' precarious situations during their own difficult times. They too fled to other countries when they faced difficult challenges in their lives. Some of their challenges were traumatic, yet they didn't give up. They kept the faith and continued the battle unabated.

I must say that in addition to the motivational lessons of my father throughout my formative years, at this crucial time of my life, I was inspired by some former African political leaders. For instance, there were times when I developed certain doubts about my own abilities and lacked confidence to keep trying. I was inspired by three popular quotes by Nelson Mandela.

I thought they wouldn't welcome me in the United States of America. Not only that, I thought it would it very difficult to cope in the States. To start all over again in a foreign country, having got used to the pretty soft approach and good life in my beloved country, Sierra Leone, was anathema. I pondered over my predicament and the inherent challenges associated with migration. Then, I reflected on one of Mandela's quotes:

"It always seems impossible until it's done."[91]

I had gone halfway in my relentless pondering on my problems. And then I thought deeply about the other bits of gossip and the feelings of self-guilt. Assuming that I failed in the United States, reflecting on my failings was the other conundrum. What would I say to myself in my quiet moments? The second quote of Mandela came to mind immediately:

"The greatest glory in living lies not in never falling, but in rising every time we fall."

With regards to the waggling of tongues at me for failing, I thought it shouldn't perturb me at all, let alone make me abandon my decision to migrate to America. Nelson Mandela said the following in his *Long Walk to Freedom*. He said this many, many times in order to inspire him to go ahead with his struggles:

"Do not judge me by my successes, judge me by how many times I fell down and got up back again."

I returned home to Sierra Leone after these brief encounters with Koroma in London. Prior to that, I had fled to the Republic of Guinea. From there, I found my way to the United States, where I applied for asylum. I encountered a lot of financial difficulties to finance my trip to the United States. I disposed of all my tangible property to purchase a ticket. Meanwhile, I left my rented premises to seek refuge in the Handala area of Conakry, the capital of Guinea.

Life in the United States was tough. Indeed, the States would grant asylum status, but unlike the UK, the asylum seeker would have to provide for his own food, lodging, and what have you. In the UK, the state provided financial assistance to those granted asylum status.

In summary, while in the UK, a relatively adequate provision would be made for the asylum seeker, including a work permit to seek employment. Once you are granted asylum status, you are free to seek employment. In the United States, you are not given a work permit until after you are granted asylum status.

I spent almost a year depending on friends and relatives, particularly my daughter Baby, for financial support. Eventually I was granted asylum status. My first job in the United States was that of a security officer. It was in a housing complex comprising six—to fourteen-story buildings.

It was a difficult job, and I had to be economical with the truth in order to secure it. I did not disclose my academic qualifications on the application form, as experience had taught me never to do so in the United States to survive as an immigrant. After only six months, I was promoted to the rank of sergeant and put in charge of the front gate. A few months later, another Sierra Leonean was employed. We did not know each other before, and I wanted to keep it that way.

One day, this Sierra Leonean was at the front gate with me, when one of his friends called to see him. When this friend saw me, he immediately became ecstatic. In Creole, he shouted my name: "Eddie Turay! How are you, sir?" I was in my security uniform. That day, my true identity was disclosed, and not long after that, I was called to the Administrative Office in order to re-visit the contents of my application forms.

After the news had reached them, I was accused of giving false information to secure a job. I did not disclose my real qualifications and my former occupation in Sierra Leone, and for that reason, I had committed an offence under US laws.

Indeed, I pleaded to my guilt but submitted that my intention was not to deliberately deceive the employer, but to secure a job to survive in the United States as an asylum seeker. I cited many instances where I applied, disclosing my qualifications, and then was turned down for being over-educated for the menial jobs I sought.

I was given a reprieve by the management and allowed to continue after I amended my application forms. After that incident, I became the most respected African in the security wing, as news went round the complex about my qualifications, both in the law and in politics.

America taught me one important lesson in life: you can make it, irrespective of your race, colour, or origin, if you work hard for what you need in life. This sat perfectly well with my philosophy in life, which I inherited from my father and mentors in my formative years.

With time, I waved good-bye to the United States of America, just as I did when I left England and the Caribbean. I returned home in 2002, re-joined the APC Party, and resumed the role of secretary general of the Party.

On my way to my homeland, the reality of all that had happened in my absence dawned on me. Not that I didn't keep in touch with my party as well as people, generally. I did so, on a daily basis, but being away creates some gaps in memories as well as in real, practical terms.

One thing about politics is that it doesn't wait for you. You have to wait for it. Politics doesn't create permanent space for you; you have to seize the opportunities as they come. And significantly, accompanying these realities is the fact that one second is a very, very long time in politics. Hence, in politics, one must make hay whilst the sun shines.

And so, in my absence people who were realists (and not just empty, euphoric dreamers) had made their mark. President Koroma had seized the initiative. While I was away in the United States, he was well established in the Party. Of course the Old Guard locked horns with the young members (the new breed reformers). The latter called themselves the "New APC Party."

Tension broke out between the Old and the New APC Party. In both camps, young uncontrollable elements of the Party confronted each other, and whenever they met, vicious fighting would erupt. It was in the midst of this situation that I returned home from the United States. The Old Guard alleged that Koroma violated the Constitution by declaring himself leader of the Party without going through an election.

The old members comprised some of the founding members, notably Alhaji Sorsoh Conteh and F. B. Turay, supported by Serry Kamal, Osho Williams, and myself (all legal practitioners), and a hosts of others, such as Dondodo (for a brief period), Ya Alimamy (logistics), Dr Labi, Dr Moses Sesay, Dr A. K. Koroma, Edward Kargbo, Birch Conteh, and a large chunk of faithful supporters across the country.

The New APC Party was substantially made up of former members of the PDP and other smaller parties.

While the hearing was on course, the members of the New APC Party declared a date for a national convention to be held in the district headquarters town of Port Loko. The Old APC Party then sought an injunction in the High Court to stop the incoming convention until the matter was settled. The injunction was initially granted but later lifted by Justice Abel Strong.

The Old Guard then appealed to the Supreme Court against the lifting of the injunction. Before the appeal hearing, Koroma's supporters in the New APC Party held the convention, and he was elected leader of the New APC Party. According to the legal record, the substantive matter was not even touched by the court.

Meanwhile, even though the matter in court was still pending, the APC Party (Old and New) joined hands together to contest the 2002 General Elections. The combined APC Party won seats in Parliament, and Koroma became the parliamentary leader of the Old and New APC Party.

Among the Old APC Party members who won seats in Parliament were Serry Kamal, Osho Williams, Jenko Stevens, Moses Sesay, and myself, and we vowed to go on with the case in court. Whenever the matter came to court, there would always be a battle between the Old APC and the New APC.

The old members, including some of the youths, felt very deeply that the advent of Ernest Bai Koroma would cause a painful marginalisation of the old members by the influx of many defecting PDP members.

While testimonies began to surface in the court, concerned members of the APC (Old and New), like retired Captain Abdul Kamara and Philip Neville, played a significant part to settle the dispute.

We held meetings in my house, one-to-one, to find a common course and end this APC versus APC saga. Alhaji Amsah, a great friend of mine, also played a significant role to reconcile Koroma and me.

After each meeting, I always consulted Osho Williams, because he was the only person who did not aspire to become a presidential candidate; Kamal, Sesay, Koroma, and I were potential aspirants. By virtue of our innate presidential demeanour, none of us was ready to step down in favour of the other for the race.

I knew this very well, and I told Koroma in our meetings that he would be my candidate if none of the old contestants stepped down. But with regards to the others, I disclosed to him that I would never step down for any of them.

As the 2007 General Elections came nearer, I knew in my heart that there was an urgent need for the sake of our country (and the overall supporters of the APC) to end this court matter. And eventually, the Political Parties Registration Commission (PPRC) was approached to see how the commission could settle this matter. We made a couple of appearances, and I knew that there would be no amicable settlement. Why? Simple! We all wanted to be president.

As a believer, I prayed and appealed to my God for direction. I did this with absolute faith and trust in the Lord.

After a few days, the answer was relayed to me by a great man of God, a foreigner in Freetown. This man of God called me and said, "Eddie, Ernest Bai Koroma will be the next leader of your country. Let us pray."

We prayed, and I felt a great relief of some sort. This was later confirmed by another man of god, a bishop, who also confirmed God's choice: Koroma.[94]

I told Williams about this; he was the only person who would not run for the presidency. I refrained from telling them the others. I knew they would never listen to me or back down.

I decided to call off the matter. It was a fact that every New APC supporter entertained the view that I was the most credible candidate, the architect who could end this unhealthy court fiasco. During this period, I had heard people in both Freetown and London quote Koroma, who said that I was his main concern.

According to my sources, he often said, "The day Eddie decides to reconcile and drop this matter, that will be the end of everything."[95]

I say this with complete modesty. I knew I was better known and appreciated for the APC leadership than any of these presidential aspirants. In the name of party unity and for the love our country, I decided to call it off and drop out of the race.

At the next PPRC meeting, before Justice Sidney Wane, I consulted Osho Williams about what I was going to say. He supported me. As soon as the meeting was called to order, I raised my hand to speak. The justice granted me that leave.

I said, "My Lord, today, I withdraw my participation in this matter. It is finished." I rose up and took Koroma by the hand and declared, "Ernest, you are the next president."

I went out outside with him. He stood by the window, and we both raised our hands to the huge crowd of supporters waiting outside. I said loudly to the crowd, "Today, our compatriots and supporters of our great party, it is finished."[96]

The announcement was received with great relief. Pandemonium, shouting, clapping, singing, and dancing simultaneously replaced the old tensions, the divisions that had hitherto set to cripple our great APC Party. We all marched to the APC headquarters, where we a large crowd was waiting for us. The slogan was "Eddie says it is finished," and before the end of the day, the party printed tens of thousands of T-shirts in honour of lasting peace in our great party.

Indeed, as was to be expected, a small number of the old APC members branded me a traitor, but I dismissed their views as the views of the devil. In their carnal knowledge, I was a traitor to them, but not in the sight of the Lord.

Destiny played its course. Man proposes but the Lord disposes. In my view, with all the conflict, the hiccups, and the lingering tempests, tranquillity ruled and the power of grace prevailed at last. The product of the party's divine reprieve became President Ernest Bai Koroma. Today, Koroma is president by the will of the Lord. So, to God be the Glory!

Reflecting back on those hectic and recalcitrant days, one fact endures. Although I withdrew from the case as demanded by divine revelations, I did so a very happy and pleased man, for two main reasons. I went down in the history of our party and country as the personality that superintended the reconciliatory course of the court matter.

I was still the incumbent secretary general at the time the matter was filed in court. The Party could not proceed to the elections while the putative leader, Koroma, was faced with a court matter. The onus was on me to withdraw the matter from the court, which I did without much ado.

With the peaceful conclusion of our internal rancour, there was now absolutely calm. We braced ourselves to continue the rejuvenation of democracy in our country. The dates for the APC primaries were announced for each district.

My first taste of humiliation by the new administration of the APC, in which I played a major role to establish its legitimacy, was the appointment of the PDP's Kemoh Sesay (a new convert to the APC Party) as chairman of the interviewing committee of Bombali District. I was billed to appear before him. What a great letdown. My first reaction was to decline to appear before him—but I was advised to proceed to the interview for two reasons:[97]

(1) If I failed to appear, it would be easier for some members of the New APC Party to say, "Eddie did not want to stand for elections." (2) If I appeared before the committee and failed the interview,

eyebrows would be raised and my supporters would confirm the muted allegations of a marginalisation of the old members of the APC.

When I appeared before Sesay, I realised at once, by his demeanour, that he had instructions to refuse me the symbol. The force of his questioning made me almost lose my composure and walk out of the hall. Indeed, to appoint him to interview me was a gross insult and a slap in my face.

These are the main reasons. Prior to that interview, I'd served the party for over ten years. I'd been a presidential candidate for the APC, a member of Parliament since 1986, and the national secretary general.

Bravely, and at a big risk, I'd stood before the NPRC Junta at the Bintumani Conference and publicly told the military to vacate power. I was sent to the Pademba Road Prison six times by the NPRC. My house was burnt to the ground for being general secretary of the APC Party only four months before the coup. I was the key architect of the peace that cleared the way, legally, for Koroma.

My decision was couched in one statement, which became a popular cliché that sustained our resolve to put it all behind us and fight: "It is finished. You are the president of Sierra Leone." We had crossed the Rubicon. And indeed it was all over, finished in good faith, and today, deservedly so, Dr Ernest Bai Koroma is the president of Sierra Leone.

Again, I have recounted these facts with no malicious feelings, but in reality, what transpired at that time was too much for me to bear. Having said that, I am much relieved and at peace with my conscience for the good works that our president and great party leaders have done in the short term of his reign. And for that, may he live long and reign over Sierra Leone, so that he will continue to lead our great party and do more for our country.

Eventually, I was awarded the APC symbol and appointed chairman of the Campaign Committee, with Paulo Conteh as my deputy. We started the campaign very well, but suddenly I became very ill. I was diagnosed with an acute prostate gland, which caused me to wear a colostomy bag.

I handed over the responsibility to Paulo. I wore the bag for well over two weeks, and my condition was deteriorating rapidly. When Koroma came to visit me in the village, I deliberately showed him the bag, and when he saw it, he nearly cried. He advised me to travel at once to Freetown and seek medical care.

I told him I would travel after the vote, which was only days away. I left my village, and on arrival in Freetown, Ernest came to my office and paid for my ticket to London. The next day, I left for the UK.

On arrival at Heathrow, my daughter was waiting for me, and she whisked me straight to see her G.P., who briefly examined me and suspected an enlarged prostate gland.

Medical tests were carried out, and a few days later, I was diagnosed cancer free. I stayed in London for a month or two and returned home, well and hearty. I must state that I owe my recovery to the Lord our God, President Ernest Bai Koroma, my beautiful and caring children, and the rest of the families and well-wishers.[99]

I must reiterate this, and I must confess that it is sincere, from the bottom of my heart. The president is a generous and caring man. I was not surprised that he financed my travel to the UK for a medical check-up.

If the president could sponsor the medical bill of his former political opponent in the 2007 presidential elections, Vice President Solomon Berewa, it is undoubtedly the case that he would render the same generosity to one of his key party officials and loyalists (and, above all, a family member).[100]

I want to reflect on the historic significance of our internal feuds and actions. Historically speaking, our internal factions did create temporary setbacks. However, these matters do happen in politics, so they were not peculiar to us.

Even in the most advanced countries in the world, including the United Kingdom, France, and the United States, there are factions. For example, in the UK, the Labour Party had factions. Tony policy, philosophy, and ideology did split the Labour Party into New Labour and Old Labour, virtually two different camps.

Not only that, even Tony Blair's New Labour camp was split due largely to personal clashes between him and his Chancellor of the Exchequer, Gordon Brown. The camps were dubbed by the press as the "Blairites" (Tony Blair's loyalists) and "Brownites" (Gordon Brown's loyalists). Prior to that, their previous rival, the Conservatives, experienced the same malaise in their party, divided into the Thatcherites and the Non-Thatcherites

Decades before, the Labour Party had suffered a serious setback as a result of the political culture of faction, splitters, breakaways, and what have you! The Social Democrats Party (SDP) was a breakaway of the old Labour Party. The Liberal Democrats is another outcome of factions.

Even now as I write this book, there is a potential splitter lingering in the current opposition Labour Party. Ed Miliband, the opposition leader, made a major announcement outlining a policy shift, which divorced him from the trade unions. Mind you, Miliband narrowly defeated his elder brother, David Miliband, because he was backed by the unions; David is an ultra-Blairite and loyalist.[101]

Having made these salient points regarding splitters, there is a significant difference in the case studies in the West: the UK, France, and the United States. In these countries, splits, factions, and breakaways occur due to ideological differences, which inform Left and Right and middle of the way policies.

On the contrary, in most of Africa, including our case study (APC) and that of the SLPP (the 2007 national conventions led to a group breaking away group from the SLPP: the PMDC, led by Charles Margai), these splits occurred largely due to personal clashes, petty jealousies, and sometimes tribalism.

All the same, based on the aforementioned case studies, the fact remains that politics is a dirty game. And splitters, divisions, and factions—differences in ideas, personal intentions, styles, philosophies, and ideologies—constitute the main body of the dirty game. Sometimes it can be healthy for politics. APC is a case in point.

The 2007 votes were cast, and the APC won the elections hands down. Ernest Bai Koroma became president. I returned home, hale and hearty and ready to work for the restoration of the APC Party in government after years in the political wilderness.

CHAPTER 15

THE POST-ELECTIONS STATE HOUSE MEETING

"A precedent embalms a principle."

Benjamin Disraeli

Due to the kind of politics practised in Africa, including my country, post-election meetings are most crucial. At these meetings, the spoils of politics are usually distributed to winners. They are about questions of winners and losers. Most significantly, inasmuch as it is about deciding the political fate of the incoming successful MPs, there are national implications.

The fact is that once MPs are elected or people are appointed to ministerial posts, they take on crucial responsibilities to justify their pedigrees. Appointed ministers carry on their shoulders the aspirations and hopes of the nation. And this is what African politicians fail to recognise. As ministers of state, we aren't answerable to ourselves but to the electorate and our nation.

We may come from different ethnic groups, regions, districts, and political parties and have different interests. All the same, we are servants of the nation. It is undoubtedly the case, because MPs are elected to serve the national interests.

However, this particular meeting in question was not about appointing cabinet ministers. That is the prerogative of the president and his group of advisors. After our successful elections in 2007, President Ernest Bai Koroma called for this special and important meeting. [102]

The meeting was called to consider parliamentary appointments. That is, appointment of MPs who would run the business of Parliament for the next five years. As stated already, all other appointments, including cabinet posts, are the exclusive rights of the president (and whoever he chooses to consult with).

The positions were:

1) Speaker of the House
2) Deputy Speaker of the House
3) Leader of the House and Government Business
4) Deputy leader of the House
5) Chief whip
6) Deputy whip

When we discussed the position of Speaker, the president suggested the name of Honourable Justice Bash Taqui. On enquiry, we learned that she was not in Freetown, so it was suggested that every effort be made to contact her immediately. It was unanimously agreed by all parties at the time.

I was offered the position of majority leader of the House and Government Business, S. B. B. Dumbuya was appointed deputy leader, Ibrahim Bundu was appointed chief whip. We all accepted our various positions.

However, when it was made clear that Justice Taqi could not make it to Freetown on time, Justice Abel Strong was suggested. I sincerely opposed him, not on the question of ability, but on his demeanour. He is very reserved, not a mixer; I believed he was too much a recluse for the likes of Parliament. I had appeared before him in court and know him very well. I opposed his appointment. Luckily, I was not alone. I was emphatically supported by Serry Kamal, Birch Conteh, and few others in the meeting.

However, Ibrahim Bundu, who proposed Justice Strong's name for the post, pleaded for him. The position of Speaker of the House is very important, and we were advised that Parliament must appoint a Speaker before its first seating. The implication was that since Honourable Taqi would not come to town on time, an alternative candidate must fill in her position. It was obvious that the tide was moving gradually in favour of Justice Strong.

I had a different idea. In my opinion, I thought that the suggestion to appoint someone else because Justice Taqi was not in town was wrong. It was not realistic and sounded hasty with a hidden undertone. In reality, a deputy speaker could have been appointed; if we wanted to avoid another round of internal conflict in our ranks, especially at a time when we were meant to celebrate our success at the polls.

If there was nothing fishy, a deputy speaker could have presided over the inaugural opening session of Parliament. After all, it was temporary duty, after which the substantive holder, Justice Taqi, could have then returned to Freetown and resumed her position as Speaker. Unfortunately, it didn't happen. This was how Justice Strong came to get the job.

Let me make it quite clear that my objections against Justice Strong were not based on his ability or his integrity. I objected to his appointment due to the fact that he was not a socialite. His interpersonal skills were poor, and the fact of the matter is that emerging from the political wilderness, we needed someone with attractive interpersonal and social skills to galvanise us around our values.

The question was his ability to unite all MPs and ministers for the good of our party. It was common knowledge among our parliamentary colleagues, as well as his fellow lawyers and justices, that he was not a unifying agent. To the extent, they gossiped freely in the corridors: "Justice Abel Strong is a loner; he never socialises or integrates with colleagues, except perhaps his drinking partners."[103]

His chambers seldom accommodated colleagues or other lawyers. On that basis, I objected to his appointment, and time has proved my views right. At the end of it all, Justice Strong was appointed, and I knew at once that a mole at that meeting had relayed to him that I objected to his appointment. Since that day, our relationship was on the rocks; he became hostile against me.

The bad taste and animosity between us had implications for our working relationship in Parliament. The leader of the House and the Speaker were supposed to work together in the preparation of the Order Papers. He seldom spoke to me, at best; he was reserved and cold towards me.

Now and again, he would travel out of the country without my knowledge. He would come back without me knowing about it. I never travelled out of the country, up to the time I left Parliament, under his watch as Speaker of the House. He put all manners of stumbling blocks in my way.

His monthly bills covering his personal provisions were sapping the allocation of parliamentary provisions. For example, toilet rolls by the dozen, wine, liquor, beer, stout, and hosts of other expenditures. They were depleting our parliamentary budget, not to mention, nearly every month he would travel out of the country.

It became an uncontrollable habit, and it had financial implications. Besides, I didn't want my reputation to be in the mud. The clerk would come and express concern about the state of our finances. He would not travel without his per-diem, while others receive it when they returned from their official trips.

149

I suggested a reduction in order to save costs and unnecessary expenditures. We were elected as MPs and appointed to run the sacred businesses of the House of Representatives with distinction. In short, the country expected us to serve as examples, as the gold standard.

Matters came to a fever pitch. How can one provide two dozen toilet rolls a month to a man living alone in his house (except with so many dogs)? I had no choice but say no. He did not like it, so our relationship plummeted even lower. Unfortunately, the parliamentary APC leadership turned against me. They were bitter and decided to support the Speaker.

To this day, everything I said about the Speaker and the APC leadership of that Parliament has proven to be correct. It is the case, in the sense that the leaders of the APC and SLPP attempted to remove him, but for the intervention of our president.

The relationship between us deteriorated to the extent that it caused concerns for President Koroma. His Excellency called a few elders to look into the matter. They included Mr Leverse, Hadson Taylor, Mr Cole, Mr Shears (all his peers) to investigate the matter. I knew at once that the scale was not balanced.

My deputy leader, S. B. B. Dumbuya, Dr Moses Sesay, Marie Yansareh, Buya Kamara, and others were to testify before this committee. The panel decided to call the Speaker and I separately. I would not know what was said by either of us. What an awkward way of settling a dispute. As a lawyer, I knew this was pre-determined, and a mole told me they all testified against me and suggested my removal from Parliament.

At the end of the hearing, Honourable Marie Yansareh phoned my number, thinking she was calling the Speaker. She said, "Mr Speaker, as per agreement, we have finished him." Then she laughed contemptuously.

I said, "Okay, Honourable Yansareh, God knows the answer. As a pastor, you will contend with your conscience." She was anxious, and within a minute, she came to my house and profusely apologised.[104]

That was not the end of the matter. Fate was to intervene once more. A few days later, Honourable Buya Kamara came to me and suggested that he would ask the president to send me to the UK as the high commissioner. I said okay; if it was the wish of His Excellency, I would be happy to leave this unworthy Parliament for eternity. I knew at once my days in Parliament were over.

The conclusion of the enquiry was never made known to me. I knew for certain those APC members—Dumbuya, Sesay, Yansareh, and Buya Kamara—testified against me to the panel.

It was their versions of events. I am a realist, a believer, as well as a lawyer. The ethics of my profession have taught me one big lesson. That lesson has profound biblical connotations: justice and fairness. They pitched their versions of events against the truth, hoping that they would buttress their conspiracy against me.

They were confident in their minds that they would succeed in dismantling me completely. Ironically, they failed to grasp a particular reality. That reality actually exposes the frailty of mankind. And this is not only prevalent in politics or our party, per se. It exists in all organisations, from corporations to government institutions. That formidable reality is the truth.

The truth is formidable and unfailing, and it serves all and sundry: all colours, all social levels, all political statuses, both genders, belief notwithstanding. I was not perturbed due to the fact that man should never be trusted, but the truth shall ever be the winner, no manner the magnitude of the deceit.

And as the Great God would have it, thankfully, President Koroma didn't fall for the lies. Instead, he stood by the truth and made the right decision. Leaders must set precedents, but they have to make sure they set the right ones. Otherwise, they will risk being on the wrong side of history.[105]

The president didn't take that risk, knowing it was not his nature. Rather, President Koroma set the right precedent in order to embalm a profound principle. It is a principle as well as virtuous character and practice worthy of emulating. Never cheat the truth, justice, and fairness.

Honourably, instead, as part and parcel of his sacred duties, he acted in defence of justice and fairness. It marked the first important meeting which marked the return of great party to power after decades in the political wilderness.

CHAPTER 16

THE ABORTIVE
PARLIAMENTARY CONSPIRACY

————◦◦◦————

"Hatred paralyses life, love releases it. Hatred confuses life, love harmonises it. Hatred darkens life, love illuminates it."

Dr Martin Luther King Jr.

Ours is a unicameral legislature in Sierra Leone. It has always being a one-chamber legislature. It was a system we inherited from the British colonial administration. This Parliament is the only legislative body in the country, unlike the bicameral legislature in other countries, including Great Britain. You can imagine why the House of Representatives is so powerful.

Whatever this powerful house decides is slated into the laws which govern both men and beasts in the land. Thus, those who steer the day-to-day administration of this great House are very important, to say the least. They hold an enviable position in the land, which is the reason why they have to stand up to highest scrutiny by their peers; partisan politics should not be a barrier.

But we are talking about politics here. It is full of intrigues, machinations, backstabbing, disappointments, and betrayers. It happens anywhere. In my case, it was one of the political paradoxes of our time. This great parliamentary conspiracy I am about to talk about in this chapter brings me back to my assertions made in the previous chapters.

In addition to the vices mentioned before, politics is not only a dirty game, it is not meant for the weak minded. This is absolutely the case because the weak would hardly survive the intrigues and conspiracies that often bedevil politics. That was what unfolded during the conspiracy against me.

This was how it all began. On 6 May 2009, a Sierra Leonean tabloid newspaper, the *African Champion*, published a report to the effect that members of Parliament, especially those in the Western Area, were involved in illegal state land transactions. The Voucher gate scandal, saga of the 1980s, did rock the nation.[106]

However, this particular one would have done solid damage to the credibility of our great party and government, had it contained a grain of truth. In that particular report, the newspaper quoted the minister of Lands and the Environment, who made his statement in the newspaper but also on FM 103 UN Radio.

This report prompted Honourable Kondeh Yapoh Conteh to raise the matter in Parliament. He said, among other things, that the integrity of Parliament was threatened and must be defended. A motion was made and passed in Parliament to summon the editor of the *African Champion* to Parliament in order to disclose the source of his allegations.

When the editor appeared in Parliament, he cited the interview given by the minister of Lands and the Environment on FM 103 UN Radio as the source of his publication. When the minister was summoned to Parliament to respond to the editor's allegation, he admitted giving the interview but added he was misunderstood. He stated that certain members of Parliament, especially those in the Western Area, were involved in illegal state land transactions.[107]

As the leader of the House and Government Business, I was shocked and very much concerned. I therefore made a motion, seconded by Honourable Musa T. Sam of the SLPP, requesting the minister to supply documents that would confirm his allegations.

The motion was unanimously passed, and the Speaker ordered the minister to produce the documents by 9 June 2009. Honourable Priddy, an MP from the Western Area, demanded the minister name names so that his credibility would be cleared. The Speaker asked the minister to be prepared to provide the names in addition to the supporting documents.

On 9 June 2009, the minister subsequently came back and submitted documents claiming that Honourable Edward M. Turay and Honourable Dauda Dumbuya, members of Parliament in the Western Area, were involved in illegal state land transactions. The Speaker of the House asked the minister to name the names in each document.

At this juncture, the drama was unfolding gradually. The minister replied that it would be unfair for him to name the members of Parliament involved. The Speaker of the House insisted that the minister must name names. The minister replied, "Mr Speaker, you cannot force me to name names."

"I will raise names based on evidence."

I am certain that the minister was forced to name names. I knew of a meeting in the Speaker's office, involving a leader of a political party and the parliamentary leadership of the APC, to cook up a conspiracy in order to embarrass me.

The minister had no choice, and on the insistence of the Speaker, he said that Dauda Dumbuya and I were involved in the alleged transactions.

The inconsistencies and inaccuracies that characterised the conspiracy were exposed immediately. A member of Parliament stood up and observed that Honourable Edward Turay (myself) did not represent the Western Area. The Speaker told him to sit down; another MP stood up, but he was told by the Speaker to sit down.

I have witnessed many parliamentary sittings when the Speaker shouted at MPs to sit down. That was clearly demeaning behaviour by the Speaker, who was not elected but appointed by Parliament. I know of a lady member of Parliament who refused to sit down when she was told to do so. It is an understatement to say that a Speaker of the House shouting at MPs demeans the dignity of the office he holds and, above all, the Sierra Leone Parliament.

Of course I was devastated; I knew the conspiracy was cooked up and orchestrated by the leadership of my party in Parliament. After this public slander, nobody from the APC parliamentary leadership comforted me, except Honourable Yapoh, Honourable Alimamy Kamara, retired Captain A. K. Kamara, Honourable Torto, and Honourable McCarthy.

This was not about differences in political parties. It was defending the integrity of Parliament and MPs. It was also aimed at cleaning dirty politics and maintaining finesse in our parliamentary proceedings. That MPs can afford to cook up unfounded stories and mount strong conspiracies against an innocent colleague because of self-interest or a personality clash was unacceptable in modern parliamentary democracy.

The SLPP leadership expressed regret; the rest of them were unconcerned. The APC MPs played into their hands, so some SLPP MPs made a meal out of it. The APC secretariat and the political leadership of the APC never said a word to me.

The whole conspiracy saga didn't surprise me at all. I knew the minister lied, and he was supported by the parliamentary leadership of my party and blessed by the Speaker (my archenemy). But like other times, whenever I find myself in trouble unfairly created by my enemies, divine grace lifts me out. Hence, due to my unfailing faith in God, I was never troubled by the event.

Interestingly, the land in question was only 8.4 town lots, not even an acre. But the minister and the press massaged the figure, put a spin on it, and magnified the acreage. Mr Minister fraudulently took the decimal point out in order to make the land read as 84 acres, which would have covered the whole area of Adonkia village.

However, the committee investigated and submitted a report to the Speaker. Unfortunately, the Speaker deliberately refused to have the report read in Parliament. This marked the twisting of the course of justice. Instead, he instructed the clerk and the deputy leader of the House not to read the report in his absence. It was one of the strategic elements of the conspiracy. Since the Speaker travels around the globe, it was obvious that the report would never be read in time.

I had to report to Honourable Philipson Kamara and Honourable Ibrahim Sorie to compel the Speaker to allow the report read in Parliament, or else I would move a motion of impeachment against the Speaker. I was determined to do so, if only that would expose and embarrass him for mounting a conspiracy against me.

The pressure on him grew, so the report was subsequently read. But it fell short of undergoing any form of debate, as it should be according to parliamentary procedure. The recommendations of the committee were never adopted and put into action, and the minister came over the radio to accuse Parliament of being corrupt and said he would never again attend Parliament, even if he was summoned to do so.

That was the end of the matter. As the committee appointed by Parliament was looking into the matter, the president invited the leadership of the APC in Parliament to the State House to discuss the scandal. His Excellency sought an answer from me. I assured him that the allegations by the minister were false and showed him the document proving the area in question was 8.4 town lots, not 84 acres.

Kamara raised his hand to say something to His Excellency. He suggested that I should be suspended from the position of leader of the House and Government Business. The president, I believe, was taken aback and said, "What for?" He spoke sharply and addressed them in the strongest terms. "The leader of the House is a lawyer, and he would defend himself."[110]

They were disappointed because they failed to drag His Excellency's name into the mud by convincing him to join their conspiratorial machinations. Without further ado, they all changed course and agreed with the decision of His Excellency. He had stated unequivocally that justice should be made to take its course.

As usual, the conspirators held their heads in shame in the presence of President Koroma. One other important thing: I have noted throughout my life that whatever plot is staged against me is always revealed either by the very people who are party to it or by a neutral, Good Samaritan. This particular failed, abortive conspiracy was no exception.

With the passage of time, a reliable source confessed to me that my colleagues had planned to recommend my suspension to His Excellency, the president, until the truth was unearthed and the matter resolved legally. During the two scenarios, the leadership and statesmanship qualities of the president were tested.

Fortunately, he justified his ingenuity as a good leader. His wisdom that guarded decisions in the two unfounded conspiracies reminded me of another of Nelson Mandela's quotes in his *Long Walk to Freedom*:

"A leader . . . is like a shepherd. He stays behind the flock, letting the most nimble go out ahead, whereupon the others follow, not realising that all along they are being directed from behind."[111]

The above qualities characterise the leadership qualities and finesse of the president. My premise for making this claim is that had it been some other leader, including the ones before him, they would have taken sides.

The contentious manner in which President Siaka Stevens and Vice President S. I. Koroma handled the problems between Thaimu Bangura and me justify my premise. On the contrary, the president took a neutral position and allowed his decisions to be guarded by the truth.

CHAPTER 17

DIPLOMATIC MISSION

———◦○◦———

"All men are caught in an inescapable network of mutuality."

Dr Martin Luther King Jr.

Before jumping into the discussion of this chapter, it may be helpful to comment on the above quote and state unequivocally that it is as true now as it was then for diplomats all over the world. It is arguably the case that corporate analysts as well as entrepreneurs have virtually reconfigured the global map, the contours of the world.

This, they argue, is due to the fact that they and the sophisticated working mechanisms they use in order to facilitate global businesses and related entrepreneurial activities have altered national and international boundaries. As a senior diplomat of my country, I don't necessarily disagree completely with these arguments. But I would like to add that it is the good will of diplomacy that has bridged the gaps which had hitherto separated the world.

Effectively, it is diplomacy that has brought together in an amicable manner those countries and leaders that were kept apart before the

Westphalia arrangements and mutual understandings and protocols. Here in the UK and Northern Ireland, as elsewhere in the world, our mission is to co-ordinate, promote, and protect the national interest of our country within the United Kingdom and the Republic of Ireland. We contribute significantly towards enhancing Sierra Leone's security and socio-economic prosperity.

It is part of our efforts and duties to boost Sierra Leone's international image and also provide efficient and quality services for Sierra Leonean residents in the United Kingdom and Northern Ireland as well as other countries. Our mission is also involved in Cyprus, Denmark, Greece, Norway, Portugal, Spain, and Sweden.[112]

Now, let us come to the theme of this chapter proper. In retrospect, I have had a succession of rough rides since I joined politics, but I have been as constant as the Northern Star. This is because I have always put my hope and trust in the Lord. I keep referring to God and the scriptures. I know that might raise a few eyebrows. Some critics might say, as a politician, I sound too godly and therefore my claims border on hypocrisy.

It is not surprising. There are lingering doubts about politicians. The doubts cut across geopolitical boundaries. And according to Tony Blair's former PR guru, Alastair Campbell, we don't play God in politics. Oh, yes, that is his opinion. But I beg to differ because in all that we do, God comes first, as He is the Alpha and Omega.

Also, I refer constantly to the Lord because of the miracles He has performed in my life. I have narrowly escaped death on many occasions, including the ones in the hands of the NPRC and AFRC.

I have repeatedly associated the name of His Excellency with the virtues of nobility, gratitude, and magnanimity. When he offered me the position of high commissioner to the UK and Northern Ireland in October 2009, I believe that he did so at the time when the Lord had so destined. Hence, I quickly accepted it gracefully.

The news of my appointment was received with scepticism by most of my supporters. It was no disregard for the decision of our great party leader and head of state. Their reservations were genuine, conceived in good faith. They wanted me to stay in Parliament where, at least, I would remain an MP until the term of Parliament expired. They were worried that the life span of a diplomat is short. It could be terminated at any time by either side, giving a month's notice.[113]

Another group of my supporters had a different view. First, they wanted me to accept the appointment due to my health. Secondly, it was a known fact in parliamentary circles that I was not the darling of the APC parliamentary leadership. Someone wanted my job. Notwithstanding all these misgivings and scepticisms, with divine help, I accepted the appointment and took up the position on 11 January 2010.

I arrived in London on a cold wintry morning. I thought things were going to be as before; each time I travelled abroad to the UK, Jamaica, and the United States, I had to join the long line of arrivals going through immigration. It was different this time. That is because the privileges accorded diplomats put them beyond such restrictions.

The moment I got off the plane, I was approached by an embassy staffer; she welcomed me politely and introduced me to a Foreign Office official. I was escorted to the diplomatic lounge, where we exchanged a few pleasantries.

On our way to my hotel, I reflected on my first arrival in the UK in 1968. The contrasts in reception this time were remarkable. When I had arrived in Liverpool, I had no one to receive me in at the dockyards. It was only by the grace of the Good Lord that someone came to my aid and put a temporary roof over my head. He also found me a job. This time around, forty years plus, here I was, in London, to be received by a Foreign Office official.

I was taken to a hotel, as the official residence was still occupied by the outgoing high commissioner. My first very day at the Sierra Leone High Commission, the next morning, was like a visit to the unknown. There was no one to receive me; the embassy door was closed. I waited for a few minutes before the security man, Michael Kamara, ushered me to my new office. It took well over two hours before the staff came in.

I was astounded to say the least. I swallowed a lump of spittle. I had to remain focused and have firm faith in my mission. I was not annoyed but sad and felt for the future of our country. All sorts of permutations lingered in my disjointed thoughts.

That we had not recovered from the vices of hate and animosity against one another, even after the decade-long civil war that brought our country to a standstill, baffled me. It brought tears in my eyes. On the other hand, I thought the unwelcoming behaviour of my compatriots could have been a genuine mistake, not done out of malice for anything.

The unwelcoming atmosphere reminded me of one of the powerful references made by the late Mother Teresa of Calcutta regarding its inherent awful feelings:

"Being unwanted, unloved, uncared for, forgotten by everybody, I think that is a much greater hunger, much greater poverty than the person who has nothing to eat."[114]

Here again is Mother Teresa on the same subject: "The hunger for love is much more difficult to remove than the hunger for bread."

Since I was not greeted by a smile, love, or hug on that day, I decided to do the opposite. I smiled broadly to everyone; after all, they were my compatriots.

I reverted to Mother Teresa of Calcutta's popular words of wisdom. In difficult, misguided times, such as this one, I summoned courage and said quietly to myself, *If we have no peace, it is because we have forgotten that we belong to each other.*

Then I further gathered myself and echoed something Mother Teresa said. In the midst of deep crises: "Let us always meet each other with smile, for the smile is the beginning of love."

And there I was, being put to the test. As I waited for my mission staff to arrive to work and meet their new high commissioner, I reflected further on how to reconcile this. I was, after all, the high commissioner, and so it was my sacred duty to reconcile my compatriots. Unity was what our nation required, and then the old, bitter grievances that caused the war would be resolved. This was not about malice; that wouldn't work. The only answer was to embark on an immediate reconciliatory strategy.

I asked what time the mission opened its doors to the public. I learnt it should be 10:00 a.m., but at that hour, no diplomatic staff had arrived. Finally, when all reported for duty, the head of chancery, Mrs Florence Bangalie, officially introduced me to the staff, and then the blackout descended over the mission.

From the office to my hotel nearby and vice versa, no one came in to see me or talk to me. From the deputy high commissioner to the diplomats, I saw no one, except the driver assigned to drive me from the hotel to the mission in the morning and back to the hotel in the afternoon. This went on for a few weeks. It seemed everybody wanted to avoid me.

However, gradually the ice melted, and later I found out that they had been given the wrong impression about me. They had been told that I was controversial. They had been told that since I was close to His Excellency, I would only create a negative portrait of the Sierra Leone High Commission.

But no matter how we paint it, the truth always has the final say. As time went by, my relationship with the staff at the high commission improved. The premonitions and the unfounded misgivings and bad stories they had heard about me had been dispelled.

The role of a diplomat is first and foremost representative of his country and government. The Sierra Leone High Commission in the UK is one of the most important diplomatic missions in the world. It entails a lot of external engagements dealing with Sierra Leone and Sierra Leone nationals staying in the UK.

My first official engagement was to pay courtesy calls to the accredited high commissioners and ambassadors to the UK and Northern Ireland. After a few months, an invitation came from Buckingham Palace via the Foreign and Commonwealth Office to present my letters of accreditation to Her Majesty the Queen.

It was one of the most distinguished occasions in my life. It was occasioned by tradition, pomp, and pageantry. The mission was full of activities; the Foreign Office Protocol Department went the extra mile to prepare me on how to address Her Majesty. The mission's role was to prepare for a reception on the day of the presentation.

I was indeed nervous; the last time I saw Her Majesty was in Makeni in 1961. She had been some distance away from me, and I was a schoolboy then, clapping for her. She was young and strikingly beautiful. This time I would see her in a completely different context. What destiny! I said to myself, *I will be very happy to see her again at Buckingham Palace, eye ball to eye ball. I will shake hands with her.*

The tears swelled, this time not around my cheeks, but inside. Then I said, "Before my father died in 1953, he made this prophecy about me shaking hands with kings and queens and heads of states. Now here I am; his prophecy has come to pass."

On the day of the presentation, the Queen's Calvary came to pick me up in a horse-driven carriage. They drove me to Buckingham Palace with my staff in another carriage behind me.

At Buckingham Palace, there was a huge crowd of people who had gathered to watch the parade, but somehow the parade was cancelled, and at that very moment, my convoy arrived, with our horse-driven carriages. The crowd went ecstatic, clapping and waving to us.

I seized the moment to wave back to them with a broad smile. The tourists from all over the world had a field day. There were plenty of snapshots as if they were billed to grace the occasion. It was just fantastic and graceful.

After we arrived at Buckingham Palace, I was ushered in to see Her Majesty. She was standing right at the top of this great and magnificent palace. I moved towards her and bowed; she welcomed me graciously. Then I bowed again and presented my letters.

She asked how President Ernest Koroma was doing. I said great, and then we entered into a lofty conversation. She was remarkable. She knew everything about Sierra Leone, even more than I know. She recalled her visit in 1961, including her visit to Makeni.

When she mentioned Makeni, it was my turn to say something. I said, "Your Majesty, do you remember those young school children in Makeni?"

She replied, "Oh yes!"

I said, "I was one of those children who clapped and chanted the words, 'God save the Queen, God save the Queen!'"

Her Majesty was visibly thrilled. She is a remarkable Queen, strong and with a fantastic memory of events all around the globe. The presentation went superbly, and my staff had the once-in-a-lifetime opportunity to shake hands with Her Majesty.

After the presentation ceremony, we organised a reception for the diplomatic community in the UK, which was well attended by my colleagues.

In the course of my duties, I also presented letters of accreditation to the kings and queens of Norway, Denmark, and Sweden and to the presidents of Cyprus, Greece, Portugal, and the Republic of Ireland. I must reiterate that they are testimonies to the prophecy of my late father.

My view about diplomacy and being a diplomat is somewhat mixed. I have heard diplomats defending their heads of states in a manner which, in my view, borders on not telling the truth. The world is so easily reached by global media, that what happens anywhere on this planet is immediate news all over the world.

But under diplomatic niceties, a diplomat has to defend his head of state and country resolutely, irrespective of the facts known by the international community. That is what diplomacy is all about. London is the hub of international diplomacy, and I enjoyed every bit of it.

Sierra Leone has a huge national diaspora, mostly resident in the southeast area of London. Take a walk to Peckham; you would be amazed to hear the altercation of Sierra Leoneans and the usual loud voices speaking in Krio, Temne, or Mende. Walk to any Sierra Leonean food shop; you will find okra, krenkren, cassava leaves, foo foo, or ogiri. These are all popular Sierra Leonean dishes.

As I mentioned before, I arrived in 2010 to take up my appointment as Sierra Leone's High Commissioner to the UK and Northern Ireland. My first official contact with the Sierra Leone community was at a meeting to introduce myself to the community. Call it a familiarisation meeting. It was well-attended.

I studied and lived in England for many years. I know my compatriots very well. We have the tendency to write anonymous letters or make statements about their own people without investigating the facts. At this meeting and subsequent ones, I made it known to them that the Sierra Leone High Commission was owned by all of us.

The high commission represents Sierra Leone and its people. It is not an APC or SLPP or PDP Party High Commission. It is not just for Temne, Mende, Loko Sosu, Kono, or any one particular ethnic group. That is why it is called the Sierra Leone High Commission. It represents Sierra Leone and her nationals abroad.

I admonished them, "If you hear anything disturbing about the mission, I implore you to call or visit the mission in order to find out the truth. We have an information attaché and other consular officials to talk to you."

They say actions speak louder than words. I introduced a political surgery for all Sierra Leoneans. Problems ranged from immigration, marital issues, and litigation. The last Friday of every month was for open visits. I secured the participation of local Sierra Leonean solicitors to render advice or solutions. For the first few months, attendance was good, and a lot of legal advice was given.

However, it became apparent that more than half of Sierra Leoneans that came to the mission were seeking financial assistance. They would ask help to pay their rents, council tax, and a host of other commitments. We tried to explain to them that the mission was not provided with such funds. What we could do was to provide them with free legal advice or possibly refer them to a solicitor to proceed further.

It became quite obvious that the meetings could not last for long, and subsequently we had to suspend them. However, we still had a system whereby consular officials proffer advice to our citizens here in the UK. My aim, and what I always admonished the staff at the high commission to do relentlessly, was to unite all Sierra Leonean nationals in the diaspora. They should inform them as well as members of the international community, including other foreign diplomats, about the national development projects the government of Sierra Leone have achieved.

Considering the sad fact that we are a nation emerging from a vicious and debilitating civil conflict, we must be proud of the strides made by the administrations of Presidents Tejan Kabbah and Ernest Bai Koroma. We must be proud of these achievements because they have to do with the nation, not individuals. It is our sacred duty as Sierra Leonean nationals and patriots to celebrate that which makes our country proud.

I spent almost three years in London, and during this period, I received awards for the outstanding high commission in 2011 and 2012. I believe quite frankly that I play my role well as high commissioner of Sierra Leone to the UK and Northern Ireland, with accreditation to the Republic of Ireland, Spain, Norway, Denmark, Sweden, Portugal, Greece, Cyprus, and Finland.

I made great friends in the United Kingdom in my capacity as Sierra Leone High Commissioner. They include friends who have manifested love for our country. I can't afford to name all of them, but I want to assure them that our country shall ever be grateful for the love they have shown us as a nation.[118]

I can't afford to conclude this book without reflecting once more on what my father prophesised would come to pass. He did so when I was only eight years old; that all he said has come to pass is still a miracle to me.

He prophesied the following:

First, I was very argumentative and smart, and I always won any complaint brought against me to my father. He clearly said during one of the complaints that I would end up to be the first lawyer in the family. And as the Lord would have it, in 1976 I was called to the English bar by Lincolns Inn in London.

Second, he confidently prophesied that I would become a leader of some sort in Sierra Leone. Indeed, to the glory of God, I became the leader of the Sierra Leone Parliament and the leader of government business for three years. I served as secretary general of the powerful APC Party from 1991 to 2002 and contested for the presidency in 1996. I would boldly say I was a part of the leadership of the APC Party, in or out of governance.

Third, and finally, the great man prophesied that I would travel abroad and would shake the hands of various kings and queens, presidents and prime ministers. Indeed, to the glory of God, I have met Her Majesty the Queen of Great Britain and Northern Ireland, as well as the kings and queens of the Scandinavian countries. I shook hands with all these sovereign monarchs. I have met the presidents of Cyprus, Portugal, Greece, and the Republic of Ireland. And there are a couple more to meet.

I have searched for the manner in which the prophecies of my late father have come true. And deep inside me, there is only one important praise to give as a mark of gratitude. Faithfully, I must confess that in all that I contemplate and do, day-in and day-out, I always say the following words in prayers before I move on:

"To the Almighty God be the Glory. Amen!"

They say God works in a mysterious ways, His wonders to foretell. He used my father, a non-believer, to prophesy what I would become, and it has come to pass. I do believe that God can do as much for you as He has done for me.

Regarding the contentious opinions people hold about politicians and the manner in which they govern, I must conclude with the following observations. Governments and their leaders are not saints. Politics and the manner in which it actually works defy all textbook lessons and theories. Over the decades and since the advent of Westphalia, the policy blueprints of most developing Third World countries have been informed mostly by textbook theories designed by the West.

The reality is that some of these policies have worked, but most of them have not. Some say that, especially since the end of the Cold War, these policies have lost their usefulness. This argument is beyond the tests of mere theories. The reason? What is the essence of policies, if they fail to impact on the needy and the vulnerable of society?

Yes, truly democracy has not served its purpose in entirety. The truism can't be overstated. Great politicians of the great nations have justified my points. Among them, Gerald R. Ford made the following observation about the failings of democracy and politics in the United States. But his observations seem generic; they apply to all countries on earth:

"In a political sense, there is one problem that currently underlies all of the others. That problem is making government sufficiently responsive to the people. If we don't make government responsive to the people, we don't make it believable, if we are to have a functioning democracy."[119]

Reflecting on the fallibility and frailty of humans and the machine we put together in a civic situation called government, Gandhi observed:

"If men were angels, no government would be necessary. If angels were to govern men, neither external nor internal controls on government would be necessary. In framing a government which is to be administered by men over men, the great difficult lies in this: you must first enable the government to control the governed, and in the next place oblige it to control itself."[120]

The thing is, there are milestones. There are contentious arguments in the ways politics has impacted developing countries for the last sixty years. I would like to reiterate that considering the sad fact that we have emerged from one of the most devastating civil wars in modern African history, we have made huge strides. The time for the blame game has past.

As Sierra Leoneans, we must be united, as nothing other than a united front, at ease with ourselves; we are more than true flesh and blood. We have gone beyond the idea of being divided into chiefdoms, districts, provinces, and municipalities in the Greater Freetown area.

We don't need any more division and divisive attitudes and machinations that brought the woes that the conflict brought upon us. It is needless to keep on apportioning blame to political parties (past and present), individual personalities, and various regimes. We should desist completely from the blame game, join hands together as a nation, and continue to forge ahead.

We can't afford to do otherwise but be united as a nation in our sprits and souls. To that end, my government and party have made huge strides, and I must say with pride and humility that we are thankful to the Sierra Leonean voters, our compatriots, that they appreciate our success stories.

It is a fact that like all other countries in the world, including the advanced, industrialised capitalist states, we have made mistakes in the past. These mistakes make us who were are. They constitute our national character. The Wars of the Roses and those during the Tudor era (1485-1603) were fought in Britain due to gross mistakes. But hundreds of years on, they have put all behind them, and they aren't ashamed of this history.

Dealing with and looking upon mistakes as taboos in once daily life is as inordinate as it is illogical. In all human endeavours, mistakes are inevitable. They are part and parcel of our day-in and day-out existence. Mistakes play an important role in the quest to attain, acquire, and defend freedom. Gandhi alluded to this perspective in every man's life and how we should relate to it:

"Freedom is not worth having if it does not include the freedom to make mistakes."[121]

They have always referred to these mistakes to make amends and forge ahead. Forging ahead requires inner peace and tranquillity. It is about harmony: harmony with our neighbours, with our communities, and among political parties, ethnicities, and regions, among every facet of our great country, Sierra Leone. Like other countries have done in the past, after making serious and deadly mistakes, Sierra Leoneans should reflect on these words of wisdom by Mahatma Gandhi: "Always aim at complete harmony of thought and word and deed. Always aim at purifying your thoughts and everything will be well."[122]

Our country has experienced the most difficult time. The 1991 civil war is a case in point. That conflict almost destroyed the entire fabric of our country. Painful of all, it almost destroyed the virtue dear to our hearts, that binds us as a nation. That virtue is love. Yes, there is still love in our hearts, but it borders on selfishness. More often than not, we love only ourselves, not our neighbours and compatriots.

True love means loving all others, not just your families and friends. What we need is the kind of special love that the Creator showered on mankind. It is that kind of love that knows neither colour nor tribe. It is not based on differences in regions, social status, or creed. Hate is our enemy and should remain so; shall it remain forevermore! It was hate that nearly destroyed our love for country and our compatriots. We can't afford to open our hearts, our doors to the attributes of hatred anymore.

Rhonda Byrne, in her extraordinary words of wisdom in relation to hate, happiness, and love, said:

"There is not a single instance in history where hate has brought joy to human beings. Hate destroys those who hold it in their minds and bodies. If humanity released all hate, fear, and resentment then no dictator could ever rise, and we would have peace on earth. Peace in our communities in the country, the world at large, can only occur through peace within each of us."

Therefore, with hate destroyed and peace and love embraced, nurtured, and loved sincerely, like the phoenix, we shall rise again.

Moreover, in this period of renewed progress, Sierra Leoneans, both at home and in the diaspora, should not forget one of the most profound and solemn declarations in the preamble of the Lome Peace Accord that was brokered and slated into law on 7 July 1999. Thankfully, it is the concrete basis of the continued, sustained peace we are enjoying in post-war Sierra Leone.

It reads:

"[Our] determination to establish sustainable peace and security, to pledge forthwith, to settle all past, present, and future differences and grievances by peaceful means, and to refrain from the threat and use of armed force to bring about any change in Sierra Leone" (A. T. Kabbah, 2010).

Post-war Sierra Leone needs infinite dialogue between politics and reasoning. It is imminent because with constant dialogue between politics and reason, especially the one based on sincerity; the prospects of conflict are zero. The saying goes, "Jaw-jaw is better than war."

And this premise was buttressed by Pope Benedict XVI when he visited the UK in September 2010.

His Holiness admonished the crowd, both the high and lowly class in London, with the following inspiring words:

"There must be a fruitful dialogue between politics and reason because the world of politics and the world of reason need each other" (Pope Benedict, 2010).

Most importantly, the dialogue between politics and reason, and forging ahead, requires a great leader. It requires a leader who can steer the ship steadily and facilitate that needed dialogue. That leader is charged with the perpetual responsibility to brave the tempests, no matter how deadly, until a safe landing is assured and accomplished. These qualities, our president proudly and graciously commands. Our great country is proud of our current president and leader.

My late, great, and visionary father prophesised that I shall one fine day shake hands with the great and the good, and that has come to pass. I am proud to state that I have not only witnessed but I was privileged to be part of the rejuvenated, new history of our great party. It is a new dawn of which we are proud and grateful to our country and the electorates.

Our great party, the APC, has just begun its second term in office, which is a remarkable hallmark of trust and faith in our party and our government. It is also an incredible manifestation of loyalty to our great leader, President Dr Ernest Bai Koroma. Together, we have made a remarkable difference in the politics and state management of post-war Sierra Leone. My fervent prayer is, may this fruitful relationship continue to be blessed by the Good Lord.

NOTES

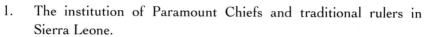

1. The institution of Paramount Chiefs and traditional rulers in Sierra Leone.
2. The relationship between the PCs and their subjects' individual loyalty, which my father's subjects owed to him and to me after his death.
3. My father was the considered the defender of the faith of his subjects.
4. My father and stepmothers once told me these stories about his supernatural powers.
5. The nature and history of these beliefs are beyond human comprehension.
6. Hegemony and wealth are often won on the battlefield. Strength is my might.
7. Acquisition of power and wealth short of dubious ways; no corruption.
8. Defined rules: hereditary was either patrilineal or matrilineal, depending on the chiefdom or kingdom.
9. See John L. Hirsch, 2001.
10. Ibid.
11. Ibid.
12. Ibid.
13. Ibid.
14. The rationale of the colonial project was divide and rule.
15. See J. A. D. Alie's *A New History of Sierra Leone.*

16. Tony Blair's comments
17. Arthur Abraham Institutions of Paramount Chieftaincy.
18. Alie, *A New History of Sierra Leone.*
19. Stories of my father about the Loko and Limba Tribal Wars.
20. Stories of my father about the supernatural powers of warlords.
21. Stories of my father.
22. Stories of my father.
23. Stories of my father.
24. Stories of my father.
25. Stories of my father about the relationship between PCs and colonial district commissioners.
26. Stories of my father.
27. Stories of my father.
28. Stories of my father.
29. Stories of my father.
30. Stories of my father.
31. Stories of my father.
32. *Things Fall Apart* by Chinua Achebe.
33. Bo Government Secondary School is one of the oldest government secondary schools for boys, established in 1906 for the education and training of the sons of PCs.
34. Wesleyan Mission was one of the earliest Christian missionaries; it promoted Christianity in Sierra Leone through education and related channels,
35. Not that Mr Koroma wasn't a competent teacher, but his verbosity about the English language and his vocabulary was comical.
36. Stories of my father.
37. The fact that I am the son of an unbeliever, an animist, makes it amazing that I was easily converted to Christianity.
38. Stories of my father.
39.
40. It was at Our Lady of Fatima that I was baptised into Catholicism.
41. Streaming was a British colonial education legacy.
42. The Queen's visit to Sierra Leone was to grace Sierra Leone's declaration of independence. She also visited the provinces.
43. A popular boat that sailed between West Africa and England.
44. "The Wind of Change," British PM Harold Macmillan.

45. I always offered prayers whenever I encountered difficulties, which I do to this day.
46. The Education Act of 1992 gave more autonomy to polytechnics to offer their own degrees under their institutions' seal.
47. One of the popular Law Inns in the UK.
48. The transatlantic slave trade involved shipping slaves from Africa to the Americas, Europe, and the Caribbean.
49. My first time in Jamaica.
50. Michael Manley was one of the most popular prime ministers the Caribbean ever had.
51. Siaka Stevens's strategy was to spot talented and qualified Sierra Leoneans in the diaspora in order to lure them to return home.
52. Stevens lured the nation into trusting him so as to remain in power indefinitely.
53. The Moyamba was the real challenge when I returned home from abroad.
54. This man was notorious for reporting civil servants to politicians in Freetown.
55. The Pa Trye Saga in Moyamba
56. The Pa Trye Saga in Moyama
57. Conversation with President Siaka Stevens about the Moyamba fiasco.
58. There was party in-fighting even when it was a one-party system.
59. The constituency was affected by ethnic, political, and personality feuds.
60. The constituency was fuelled by extreme violence.
61. *"Puawei"* in the Mende language means grey or silver hair. Dr Banya had grown grey under the weight of the workload of two cabinet ministries: Finance and Economic Development. The pressure of Sierra Leone hosting the OAU also added to the pressure.
62. President Siaka Stevens admonished Bangura and I to come to our senses.
63. This was President Stevens's appeasement strategy to me after disappointing me in the first instance.
64. A popular proverb and a famous political cliché. Patience is important for lasting success.

65. There was a bond of absolute trust between my father and his loyal subjects.

66. There were increased boundaries in the North as in other parts of the country to create quantitative parity.

67. Abraham Taqi was a veteran journalist and politician. He eventually fell out with President Siaka Stevens and was charged with treason against the president. This was part of his statement proclaiming his innocence.

68. The wider ramification of the Cold War led to the West ignoring the political and socio-economic problems of Africa and most of the Third World.

69. The 1991 Constitution was written by Dr P. L. Tucker. I was a member of the Constitution Committee. It paved the way for multiparty democracy and brought an end to the last bastion of the Old Guard.

70. Presentation at FBC, University of Sierra Leone, with other party leaders. I drew the line between the Old and Privileged APC and the New APC we were bent on building. Members of other political parties, including those who deserted the almost defunct Old APC, were at the presentation

71. Presentation at FBC, University of Sierra Leone.

72. Bambay Kamara was Sierra Leone's police commissioner, a staunch APC member and loyalist.

73. Filie Faboy was a strategic appointment by the APC, being an easterner. He was a unifying candidate

74. Mr John Karimu was minister of Finance in the NPRC Military Junta; he became the leader of the political party that was formed in the image and likeness of the NPRC. He served as chairman of the National Revenue Authority.

75. Old Guards of the APC: Siaka Stevens, his inner circle, and privileged loyalists.

76. The number of my prison room at the Pademba Road Prison after I was arrested by the military junta.

77. Memories about my life in prison.

78. Leaflets critical of the military junta. Any article they published was associated with me, for which the junta detained me at Pademba Road Prison many times.

79. The admonitions of my late father, Paramount Chief Kande Turay.
80. News of my release from prison created consternation among my supporters and my family. When I was locked up in prison, they thought I would be executed by the junta. Little did they know that I would be saved and released by the Lord!
81. The height of the junta's atrocities, a grotesque human rights abuse.
82. The important conferences held in Bintumani to decide whether to conduct elections and end the war or wait until end of war to hold elections. Most people thought it was a political ploy by the NPRC Junta, who favoured ending the war before elections, so that they would stay in power indefinitely. It was counterproductive, but the voice of the populace won the day.
83. My speech at the Bintumani Conference. I emphasised the significant differences between the Old and New APC, which I stood for. I also supported the voice and demands of the populace and the majority of those at the conference.
84. See self-explanatory speech above.
85. The Nigeria high commissioner was simply trying to point out to me the dangerous route I took in the interest of democratic renewal.
86. The admonitions of my father.
87. See the self-explanatory comments above.
88. See the self-explanatory revelation by the Western diplomat who preferred to remain anonymous.
89. The impressive leadership qualities of President Ernest Bai Koroma.
90. Nelson Mandela's popular quotes.
91. Ibid.
92. Ibid.
93. The bishop revealed to me that Ernest Bai Koroma will be the choice of the APC Party and the people of Sierra Leone.
94. The dignified qualities of President Ernest Bai Koroma.
95. My inspired comment of unifying the party behind the chosen candidate, Ernest Bai Koroma.
96. These were trying times. How could politics be so cruel?
97. My declaration for President Ernest Bai Koroma.

98. This underpins Koroma's generosity. But for the interventions of him, the Lord, and my caring children, I would have died.

99. This underpins the generosity of the vice president, my opponent during the 2007 elections. Solomon Berewa revealed the same in his book, *A New Perspective on Governance, Leadership, Conflict and Nation Building in Sierra Leone* (2011).

100. Party in-fighting is part and parcel of the turbulent game of politics, regardless geopolitical differences.

101. Not a meeting to appoint cabinet posts but to select the people who would run the parliamentary businesses. It was at this meeting that I discovered that some members were still up to their usual games: intrigues, conspiracy, undermining colleagues.

102. Justices Abel Strong and Taqi were the key candidates. Initially, the lot fell on Justice Taqi.

103. The discovery of my conspirators reinforced my comments at the FBC presentations: the faction poison and the nemesis of our party.

104. Testimony to President Kamara's leadership qualities.

105. For the second time, my party colleagues conspired against me.

106. In Africa, the moment allegations are made against politicians, the media has a field day.

107. Self-explanatory.

108. Self-explanatory.

109. Another significant testimony to President Kamara's leadership qualities.

110. Nelson Mandela's popular quotes.

111. The official remits of the Sierra Leone High Commissioner to the UK and Ireland.

112. My constituents were anxious that being far away from them would create a gulf between us.

113. Popular quotes by Mother Teresa of Calcutta.

114. Ibid.

115. Ibid.

116. Self-explanatory.

117. Self-explanatory.

118. That United Kingdom, especially the Labour Government under Blair, stood by us even before I was stationed here demands our relentless gratitude as a nation.

119. Popular quotes by Gerald R. Ford.
120. Popular quotes by Gandhi.
121. Ibid.
122. Ibid.
123. Ibid.

SELECTED BIBLIOGRAPHY

—◦◦◦—

1. Alie, J. A. D. (1990). *A New History of Sierra Leone*. London: Macmillan.
2. Berewa, S. E. (2011). *A New Perspective on Governance, Leadership, Conflict and Nation Building in Sierra Leone*. London, Indianapolis: AuthorHouse.
3. Keen, D. (2005). *Conflict and Collusion in Sierra Leone*. Oxford: James Curry for International Peace Academy.
4. Ellis, S. (1996). "Analysing Africa's Wars." Paper presented at the UCL.
5. Thomson, A. (2004). *Introduction to African Politics*. Routledge Taylor Francis Groups.
6. Bundu, A. (2001). *Democracy by Force?* Universal Publishers.
7. Kabbah, A. T. (2010). *Coming Back from the Brink in Sierra Leone*. Accra, Ghana: EPP Books Services.
8. Achebe, C. (1958). *Things Fall Apart*. African Writers Series.
9. Harris, D. (2012). *Civil War and Democracy in West Africa*. London, New York: IB Tauris & Co.
10. Otunnu, O. A., and Michael W. Doyle (1998). *Peace Making and Peacekeeping for the New Century*. Rowman & Littlefield Publishers.
11. Hirsch, J. L. (2001). *Sierra Leone: Diamonds and the Struggle for Democracy*. International Peace Academy Occasional Paper Series, Lynne Rienner Publishers.
12. Abdullah, Ibrahim (1998). *Bush Path to Destruction: The Origins and Character of the Revolutionary United Front*.

13. Wundah, M. N. (2004). *Sunset in Sierra Leone*. Sussex, England: The Book Guild Ltd.
14. Wundah, M. N. (2011). *Landscaping Sierra Leone: Third Way Politics in the Mould of Attitudinal and Behaviour Change*. Red Lead Press.
15. Stevens, S. (1984). *What Life Has Taught Me*. Sierra Leone.
16. Bergner, D. (2004). *Soldiers of Light*. Penguin Books.
17. Wyse, A. (1989). *The Krio of Sierra Leone: An Interpretive History*. C. Hurst & Co.
18. Sekgoma, Gilbert A. (1981). *Decolonisation in Sierra Leone 1938-1961*. Dalhousie.
19. Benjamin Disraeli: 1804-1881.
20. Mahatma Gandhi: 1869-1948.
21. Martin Luther King Jr.: 1929-1968.
22. Mother Teresa of Calcutta: 1910-1997.
23. Mother Teresa's Message to Fourth UN Women's Conference.
24. Brooks, George (1993). *Landlords and Strangers: Ecology, Society, and Trade in Western Africa, 1000-1630*.
25. Rodney, Walter (1970). *A History of Upper Guinea Coast, 1545-1800*. Oxford: Clarendon Press.
26. Wylie, Kenneth (1977). *The Political Kingdoms of the Temne: Temne Government in Sierra Leone 1825-1910*. New York: African Publishing Company.
27. Pope Benedict XVI (2010). Visit to the UK, 13-19 September 2010.
28. Susan Neiman (2009).

Websites

1. His Excellency Dr Siaka Probyn Stevens: www.siakastevens.org/categoryMyLife
2. The APC Party: http: www.Siakastevens.org
3. Temne People: Wikipedia
4. Assessment for Temne in Sierra Leone
5. Temne Masks and Headdresses, Sierra Leone
6. www.Quotations page.com
7. www.Slhc.uk.org.uk
8. www.ewnt.com

ABOUT THE AUTHOR

His Excellency Ambassador Eddie M. Turay is Sierra Leone's High Commissioner to the United Kingdom and eight other West European Countries. Ambassador Turay is a British trained and qualified lawyer. He enrolled at Inns of Courts School of Law and graduated with Honours Degree in law. He was called to the English Bar by Lincolns Inn in 1976.

After a few months in England, he secured a job with the Jamaica Judiciary as Deputy Clerk of Courts in 1976. He worked in Montego Bay and was promoted to the post of Clerk of Courts.

HE Ambassador Eddie M. Turay was lured by the late President Siaka Stevens to return home and serve his motherland. He was appointed Resident Magistrate for Moyamba and Bonthe Districts in the Southern Province, with residence in Moyamba Town.

Ambassador Turay later went into politics, served as MP and National Secretary General of the All Peoples' Congress Party (APC), during the party's trying days in the 1990s. He contested for the leadership of the party prior to the 2007 Parliamentary and Presidential Elections against the current President and leader of the party, His Excellency, Dr Ernest Bai Koroma and others. Gracefully, he withdrew from the race in favour of the latter, who he perceived a true winner and leader.

After the elections, he was appointed by His Excellency, the President of Sierra Leone Dr Ernest Bai Korma to serve in his current position as Sierra Leone's High Commissioner to the UK and eight other West European Countries. He has served his country in this position since with distinction and finesse.

His Excellency Ambassador Eddie M. Turay has a very supportive family, he is proud of at all time. He has also made many good friends at home and abroad.

This is Ambassador Turay's first book, but it is one with a difference. It is significantly different because, this book marks him out as the first serving Sierra Leonean senior diplomat with ambassadorial status to write a book with amazing story line, analytical bents and honest personal revelations.

Lightning Source UK Ltd.
Milton Keynes UK
UKOW05f0859221013

219519UK00002B/53/P